UNITY FROM ZERO TO PROFICIENCY (INTERMEDIATE)

Second Edition

A step-by-step guide to programming your game in C#.

Patrick Felicia

Unity From Zero to Proficiency
(Intermediate)

Second Edition

Copyright © 2018 Patrick Felicia

All rights reserved. No part of this book may be reproduced, stored in retrieval systems, or transmitted in any form or by any means, without the prior written permission of the publisher (Patrick Felicia), except in the case of brief quotations embedded in critical articles or reviews.

Every effort has been made in the preparation of this book to ensure the accuracy of the information presented. However, the information contained in this book is sold without warranty, either expressed or implied. Neither the author and its dealers and distributors will be held liable for any damages caused or alleged to be caused directly or indirectly by this book.

First published: April 2016

Second Edition published: February 2018

Published by Patrick Felicia

CREDITS

Author: Patrick Felicia

ABOUT THE AUTHOR

Patrick Felicia is a **lecturer and researcher** at Waterford Institute of Technology, where he teaches and supervises undergraduate and postgraduate students. He obtained his MSc in Multimedia Technology in 2003 and PhD in Computer Science in 2009 from University College Cork, Ireland. He has published several books and articles on the use of video games for educational purposes, including the Handbook of Research on Improving Learning and Motivation through Educational Games: Multidisciplinary Approaches (published by IGI), and Digital Games in Schools: a Handbook for Teachers, published by European Schoolnet. Patrick is also the Editor-in-chief of the **International Journal of Game-Based Learning (IJGBL)**, and the Conference Director of the **Irish Conference on Game-Based Learning**, a popular conference on games and learning organized throughout Ireland.

Support and Resources for this Book + Free Book

As a new reader of my book series, and to thank you for choosing this book, I would like to offer you a free book. So, to receive your book, just email me at **learntocreategames@gmail.com** with a screenshot of your Amazon receipt and I will send you a **FREE** copy of the book "**A Quick Guide to Procedural Level Generation**" (worth $3), a book that will extend the content provided in this book and help you to create levels faster for your games. After receiving your free book, you will also receive weekly updates and FREE tutorials on Unity 2017.

>> CLAIM YOUR FREE BOOK <<

To complete the activities presented in this book you need to download the startup pack on the companion website; it consists of free resources that you will need to complete your projects, including bonus material that will help you along the way (e.g., cheat sheets, introductory videos, code samples, and much more).

These resources also include the final completed project so that you can see how your project should look like in the end.

Amongst other things, the resources for this book include:

- All the C# scripts used in this book.
- Cheat sheets with tips on how to use Unity.
- 3D characters and animation that you can use in Unity.
- A library of over 40 tutorials (video or text).

To download these resources, please do the following:

- Open the following link: **http://learntocreategames.com/books/**
- Select this book ("**Unity from Zero to Proficiency - Intermediate**").
- On the new page, click on the link labelled "**Book Files**", or scroll down to the bottom of the page.

- In the section called "**Download your Free Resource Pack**", enter your email address and your first name, and click on the button labeled "**Yes, I want to receive my bonus pack**".

- After a few seconds, you should receive a link to your free start-up pack.

- When you receive the link, you can download all the resources to your computer.

This book is dedicated to Helena & Mathis

TABLE OF CONTENTS

1 Introduction to Programming in C# 17
    Why use C# instead of JavaScript 18
    Introduction 19
    Statements 21
    Comments 23
    Variables 25
    Arrays 27
    Constants 30
    Operators 32
    Conditional statements 33
    Switch Statements 34
    Loops 36
    Classes 39
    Defining a class 40
    Accessing class members and variables 41
    Constructors 45
    Destructors 47
    Static members of a class 48
    Inheritance 51
    Methods 55
    Accessing methods and access modifiers 57
    Common methods 58
    Scope of variables 59
    Events 61
    Polymorphism (general concepts) 62
    Dynamic polymorphism 63
    Workflow to create a script 65
    How scripts are compiled 66
    Coding Convention 67
    A few things to remember when you create a script (checklist) 68
    Level Roundup 70

2 Creating your First Script 74
    Quick overview of the interface 75
    Getting started 77
    Creating your first method 88
    Creating your own class 94
    Common errors and their meaning 99
    Best practices 102
    Level Roundup 103

3 Adding Simple AI 107
    Resources necessary for this chapter 108
    Instantiating projectiles 109

    Finishing our first game 133
    Detecting when the player has reached the end of the game 145
    Level Roundup 148

4 Creating and Managing Weapons 153
    Setting-up the environment 155
    Detecting objects ahead using raycasting 158
    Creating a weapon 163
    Building a weapon management system with arrays 174
    Managing the collection of ammunitions 185
    Creating a grenade launcher 190
    Level Roundup 199

5 Using Finite State Machines 203
    Introduction to finite state machines 204
    Getting started with finite-state machines in Unity 205
    Controlling an Animator Controller from a C# script 212
    Linking transitions to the movement of objects 217
    Using Animated Characters with Mecanim 223
    Making the NPC smarter 233
    Adding weapons to the player 238
    Adding animations for more realism 243
    Applying damage to the player 248
    Using Dot products for more accuracy 261
    Adding a screen flash when the player is hit 268
    Creating new prefabs 273
    Level Roundup 274

6 Putting it all together 278
    Setting-up the environment manually 279
    Setting-up the environment through scripting 286
    Level Roundup 293

7 Frequently Asked Questions 294
    C# Scripts 295
    Rigid Bodies 297
    Using prefabs 298
    Finite State Machines 299
    Navmesh Navigation 300

8 Thank you 301

PREFACE

After teaching Unity for over 4 years, I always thought it could be great to find a book that could get my students started with Unity in a few hours and that showed them how to master the core functionalities offered by this fantastic software.

Many of the books that I found were too short and did not provide enough details on the why behind the actions recommended and taken; other books were highly theoretical, and I found that they lacked practicality and that they would not get my students' full attention. In addition, I often found that game development may be preferred by those with a programming background but that those with an Arts background, even if they wanted to get to know how to create games, often had to face the issue of learning to code for the first time.

As a result, I started to consider a format that would cover both: be approachable (even to the students with no programming background), keep students highly motivated and involved using an interesting project, cover the core functionalities available in Unity to get started with game programming, provide answers to common questions, and also provide, if need be, a considerable amount of details for some topics.

This book series entitled **From Zero to Proficiency** does just this. In this book series, you have the opportunity to play around with Unity's core features, and essentially those that will make it possible to create an interesting 3D game rapidly. After reading this book series, you should find it easier to use Unity and its core functionalities.

This book series assumes no prior knowledge on the part of the reader, and it will get you started on Unity so that you quickly master all the wonderful features that this software provides by going through an easy learning curve. By completing each chapter, and by following step-by-step instructions, you will progressively improve your skills, become more proficient in Unity, and create a survival game using Unity's core features in terms of programming (C# and JavaScript), game design, and drag and drop features.

In addition to understanding and being able to master Unity's core features, you will also create a game that includes many of the common techniques found in video games, including: level design, object creation, textures, collision detection, lights, weapon creation, character animations, particles, artificial intelligence, and a user interface.

Throughout this book series, you will create a game that includes both indoor and outdoor environments, where the player needs to finds its way out of the former through tunnels, escalators, traps, and other challenges, avoid or eliminate enemies using weapons (i.e., gun or grenades), drive a car or pilot an aircraft.

You will learn how to create customized menus and simple user interfaces using Unity's UI system, and animate and give (artificial) intelligence to Non-Player Characters (NPCs) who will be able to follow your character using Mecanim and Navmesh navigation.

Content Covered by this Book

Chapter 1, Introduction to C#, provides an introduction to C# and to core principles that will help you to get started. It explains key programming concepts such as variables, variable types, polymorphism, constructors, or methods as well as best practices for C# programming within Unity.

Chapter 2, Creating your First Script, helps you to code your first script in C#. It explains common coding mistakes and errors in Unity, and how to avoid them easily. It also goes through some common error messages for beginners, and explains what they mean and how they can be avoided easily.

Chapter 3, Adding Simple AI, gets you to use C# for the creation of a simple launcher. You will learn to instantiate, use and control Rigidbody objects from your script as well as creating explosions.

Chapter 4, Creating and Managing Weapons, explains how you can create and manage weapons using a simple inventory system. You will create an automatic gun and a grenade launcher, manage the collection of ammunitions, and also implement a user interface to keep track of ammunitions. In addition, you will also learn how to include these as prefabs, so that they can be reused in other levels, and to save you some coding too.

Chapter 5, Using Finite State Machines, provides an in-depth explanation of how to create and use Finite State Machines (FSM) in Unity. You will create your FSM and use it to control the behavior and movement of an animated Non-Player Character. You will also learn how to employ NavMesh navigation so that your animated NPCs can navigate easily within the scene to either follow the player or go to a specific location. Finally, you will learn how to optimize your assets so that they can be reused seamlessly in other scenes with no or little changes.

Chapter 6, Putting it All Together, makes it possible to combine the skills you have acquired in the previous chapters, and to reuse and combine all the objects that you have created so far (e.g., NPCs, weapons, inventory syetems, ammunitions, etc.), and the concepts (e.g., FSM, NavMesh, RigidBody components, User Interface, etc.) that you have mastered, to create a fully functional level. You will also get to learn how to generate a maze (or a game level) dynamically from your code.

Chapter 7 provides answers to Frequently Asked Questions (FAQs) related to the topics covered in this book (e.g., FSM, NavMesh, Rigiddbody components, or Artificial Intelligence). It also provides links to additional exclusive video tutorials that can help you with some of your questions.

Chapter 8 summarizes the topics covered in the book and provides you with more information on the next steps.

WHAT YOU NEED TO USE THIS BOOK

To complete the project presented in this book, you only need Unity 5.0, Unity 2017, or a more recent version, and to also ensure that your computer and its operating system comply with Unity's requirements. Unity can be downloaded from the official website (**http://www.unity3d.com/download**), and before downloading, you can check that your computer is up to scratch on the following page: **http://www.unity3d.com/unity/system-requirements**. At the time of writing this book, the following operating systems are supported by Unity for development: Windows XP (i.e., SP2+, 7 SP1+), Windows 8, and Mac OS X 10.6+. In terms of graphics card, most cards produced after 2004 should be suitable.

In terms of computer skills, all knowledge introduced in this book will assume no prior programming experience from the reader. So for now, you only need to be able to perform common computer tasks, such as downloading items, opening and saving files, be comfortable with dragging and dropping items and typing, and relatively comfortable with Unity's interface. This being said, because the focus of this book is on scripting, and while all steps are explained step-by-step, you may need to be relatively comfortable with Unity's interface, as well as creating and transforming objects.

So, if you would prefer to become more comfortable with Unity prior to starting scripting, you can download the first book in the series called **Unity From Zero to Proficiency (Foundations)** or its sequel called **Unity from Zero to Proficiency (Beginner)**. These books cover most of the shortcuts and views available in Unity, as well as how to perform common tasks in Unity such as creating objects, transforming objects, importing assets, using navigation controllers, creating scripts or exporting the game to the web. They also explain some of the key features available in Unity along with good coding practices.

WHO THIS BOOK IS FOR

If you can answer **yes** to all these questions, then this book is for you:

1. Are you a total beginner in Unity or programming?

2. Would you like to become proficient in the core functionalities offered by Unity?

3. Would you like to teach students or help your child to understand how to create games, using coding in C#?

4. Would you like to start creating great games?

5. Although you may have had some prior exposure to Unity, would you like to delve more into Unity and understand its core functionalities in more detail?

WHO THIS BOOK IS NOT FOR

If you can answer yes to all these questions, then this book is **not** for you:

1. Can you already code in C# and implement Artificial Intelligence or manage animated characters through coding in Unity?

2. Can you already easily code a 3D game with Unity, using C#, with built-in objects, controllers, cameras, lights, terrains, AI-driven non-player characters, and weapons?

3. Are you looking for a reference book on Unity programming?

4. Are you an experienced (or at least advanced) Unity user?

If you can answer yes to all four questions, you may instead look for the next book in the series called Unity from Zero to Proficiency (Advanced). To see the content and the topics covered in this book, you can check the official website (http://www.learntocreategames.com/books/).

How you will Learn from this Book

Because all students learn differently and have different expectations of a course, this book is designed to ensure that all readers find a learning mode that suits them. Therefore, it includes the following:

- A list of the learning objectives at the start of each chapter so that readers have a snapshot of the skills that will be covered.

- Each section includes an overview of the activities covered.

- Many of the activities are step-by-step, and learners are also given the opportunity to engage in deeper learning and problem-solving skills through the challenges offered at the end of each chapter.

- Each chapter ends-up with a quiz and challenges through which you can put your skills (and knowledge acquired) into practice, and see how much you know. Challenges consist in coding, debugging, or creating new features based on the knowledge that you have acquired in the chapter.

- The book focuses on the core skills that you need; some sections also go into more detail; however, once concepts have been explained, links are provided to additional resources, where necessary.

- The code is introduced progressively and is explained in detail.

- You also gain access to several videos that help you along the way, especially for the most challenging topics.

Format of each Chapter and Writing Conventions

Throughout this book, and to make reading and learning easier, text formatting and icons will be used to highlight parts of the information provided and to make it more readable.

The full solution for the project presented in this book is available for download on the official website (http://learntocreategames.com/books/). So if you need to skip a section, you can do so; you can also download the solution for the previous chapter that you have skipped.

SPECIAL NOTES

Each chapter includes resource sections, so that you can further your understanding and mastery of Unity; these include:

- A quiz for each chapter: these quizzes usually include 10 questions that test your knowledge of the topics covered throughout the chapter. The solutions are provided on the companion website.

- A checklist: it consists of between 5 and 10 key concepts and skills that you need to be comfortable with before progressing to the next chapter.

- Challenges: each chapter includes a challenge section where you are asked to combine your skills to solve a particular problem.

Author's notes appear as described below:

> Author's suggestions appear in this box.

Code appears as described below:

```
public int score;
public string playersName = "Sam";
```

Checklists that include the important points covered in the chapter appear as described below:

- Item1 for check list
- Item2 for check list
- Item3 for check list

How Can You Learn Best from this Book

- **Talk to your friends about what you are doing.**

  We often think that we understand a topic until we have to explain it to friends and answer their questions. By explaining your different projects, what you just learned will become clearer to you.

- **Do the exercises.**

  All chapters include exercises that will help you to learn by doing. In other words, by completing these exercises, you will be able to better understand the topic and gain practical skills (i.e., rather than just reading).

- **Don't be afraid of making mistakes.**

  I usually tell my students that making mistakes is part of the learning process; the more mistakes you make and the more opportunities you have for learning. At the start, you may find the errors disconcerting, or that the engine does not work as expected until you understand what went wrong.

- **Export your games early.**

  It is always great to build and export your first game. Even if it is rather simple, it is always good to see it in a browser and to be able to share it with you friends.

- **Learn in chunks.**

  It may be disconcerting to go through five or six chapters straight, as it may lower your motivation. Instead, give yourself enough time to learn, go at your own pace, and learn in small units (e.g., between 15 and 20 minutes per day). This will do at least two things for you: it will give your brain the time to "digest" the information that you have just learned, so that you can start fresh the following day. It will also make sure that you don't "burn-out" and that you keep your motivation levels high.

FEEDBACK

While I have done everything possible to produce a book of high quality and value, I always appreciate feedback from readers so that the book can be improved accordingly. If you would like to give feedback, you can email me at **learntocreategames@gmail.com**.

Downloading the Solutions for the Book

To complete the activities presented in this book you need to download the startup pack on the companion website; it consists of free resources that you will need to complete your projects, including bonus material that will help you along the way (e.g., cheat sheets, introductory videos, code samples, and much more).

These resources also include the final completed project so that you can see how your project should look like in the end.

Amongst other things, the resources for this book include:

- All the C# scripts used in this book.
- Cheat sheets with tips on how to use Unity.
- 3D characters and animation that you can use in Unity.
- A library of over 40 tutorials (video or text).

To download these resources, please do the following:

- Open the following link: **http://learntocreategames.com/books/**
- Select this book ("**Unity from Zero to Proficiency - Intermediate**").
- On the new page, click on the link labelled "**Book Files**", or scroll down to the bottom of the page.
- In the section called "**Download your Free Resource Pack**", enter your email address and your first name, and click on the button labeled "**Yes, I want to receive my bonus pack**".
- After a few seconds, you should receive a link to your free start-up pack.

When you receive the link, you can download all the resources to your computer.

IMPROVING THE BOOK

Although great care was taken in checking the content of this book, I am human, and some errors could remain in the book. As a result, it would be great if you could let me know of any issue or error you may have come across in this book, so that it can be solved and the book updated accordingly. To report an error, you can email me (**learntocreategames@gmail.com**) with the following information:

- Name of the book.

- The page or section where the error was detected.

- Describe the error and also what you think the correction should be.

Once your email is received, the error will be checked, and, in the case of a valid error, it will be corrected and the book page will be updated to reflect the changes accordingly.

SUPPORTING THE AUTHOR

A lot of work has gone into this book and it is the fruit of long hours of preparation, brainstorming, and finally writing. As a result, I would ask that you do not distribute any illegal copies of this book.

This means that if a friend wants a copy of this book, s/he will have to buy it through the official channels (i.e., through Amazon, lulu.com, or the book's official website: **http://www.learntocreategames.com/books/**).

If some of your friends are interested in the book, you can refer them to the book's official website (**http://www.learntocreategames.com/books/**) where they can either buy the book, enter a monthly draw to be in for a chance of receiving a free copy of the book, or to be notified of future promotional offers.

1
INTRODUCTION TO PROGRAMMING IN C#

In this section we will discover C# programming principles and concepts, so that you can start programming in the next chapter. If you have already coded using C# (or a similar language), you can skip this chapter.

After completing this chapter you will be able to:

- Understand key differences between UnityScript and C#.
- Understand the reasons why you need to consider C#.
- Understand object-oriented programming (OOP) concepts when coding in C#.
- Get used to and understand the concepts of variables, methods, and scope.
- Understand key best practices for coding, particularly in C#.
- Understand conditional statements and decision making structures.
- Understand the concept of loops.

WHY USE C# INSTEAD OF JAVASCRIPT

From Unity 2017 onwards, UnityScript is no longer supported in Unity. In addition, by learning C# within Unity, you get to discover a new language that is object-oriented, relatively easy to learn, and with strong resemblances with Java (another widespread object-oriented language). So while JavaScript makes sense at the start of your journey through Unity, it is also a good idea to move on to C# and develop skills that you will be able to transfer to other platforms and programming languages. Another advantage of using C# is that it may be a good asset if you would like to pursue a career in the gaming industry, as many gaming companies use this programming language.

INTRODUCTION

When scripting in Unity, you are communicating with the Game Engine and asking it to perform actions. To communicate with the system, you are using a language or a set of words bound by a syntax that the computer and you know. This language consists of keywords, key phrases, and a syntax that ensures that the instructions are understood properly. In computer science, this sentence needs to be exact, precise, unambiguous, and with a correct syntax. In other words, it needs to be **exact**. The syntax is a set of rules that are followed when writing code in C# (as for JavaScript). In addition to its syntax, C# programming also uses classes; so your scripts will be saved as classes.

In the next section, we will learn how to use this syntax. If you have already coded in JavaScript, some of the information provided in the rest of this chapter may look familiar and this prior exposure to JavaScript will definitely help you. This being said, UnityScript and C#, despite some relative similarities, are quite different in many aspects (e.g., variable declaration, function declaration, etc.).

When scripting in C#, you will be using a combination of the following:

- Classes.
- Objects.
- Statements.
- Comments.
- Variables.
- Constants.
- Operators.
- Assignments.
- Data types.
- Methods.
- Decision making structures.
- Loops.
- Inheritance (more advanced).
- Polymorphism (more advanced).
- Operator overloading (more advanced).

- Interfaces.
- Name spaces.
- Events.
- Comparisons.
- Type conversions.
- Reserved words.
- Messages to the console windows.
- Declarations.
- Calls to methods.

The list may look a bit intimidating but, not to worry, we will explore these in the next sections, and you will get to know and use them smoothly using hands-on examples.

STATEMENTS

When you write a piece of C# code, you need to tell the system to execute your instructions (e.g., print information) using statements. A statement is literally an order or something you ask the system to do. For example, in the next line of code, the statement will tell Unity to print a message in the **Console** window:

```
print ("Hello Word");
```

When writing statements, there are a few rules that you need to know:

- Order of statements: each statement is executed in the order it appears in the script. For example, in the next example, the code will print **hello**, then **world;** this is because the associated statements are in that particular sequence.

```
print ("hello");
print ("world");
```

- Statements are separated by **semi-colons** (i.e., semi-colon at the end of each statement).

> Note that several statements can be added on the same line, as long as they are separated by a semi-colon.

- For example the next line of code has a correct syntax.

```
print("hello");print ("world");
```

- Multiple spaces are ignored for statements; however, it is good practice to add spaces around the operators such as +, -, /, or % for clarity. For example, in the next example, we say that **a** is equal to **b**. There is a space both before and after the operator =.

```
a = b;
```

- Statements to be executed together (e.g., based on the same condition) can be grouped using what is usually referred to as **code blocks**. In C# (as for JavaScript), code blocks are symbolized by curly brackets (e.g., { or }). So, in other words, if you needed to group several statements, we would include them all within the same curly brackets, as follows:

```
{
    print ("hello stranger!");
    print ("today, we will learn about scripting");
}
```

As we have seen earlier, a statement usually employs or starts with a keyword (i.e., a word that the computer knows). Each of these keywords has a specific purpose and the most common ones (at this stage) are used for:

Introduction to Programming in C#

- Printing a message in the **Console** window: the keyword is **print**.

- Declaring a variable: the keyword depends on the type of variable (e.g., **int** for integers, **string** for text, **bool** for Boolean variables, etc.) and we will see more about this in the next sections.

- Declaring a method: the keyword depends on the type of the data returned by the method. For example, in C#, the name of a method is preceded by the keyword **int** when the method returns an **integer**, **string** when the method returns a **string**, or **void** when the method does not return any information.

> What is called a **method** in C# is what used to be called a function in UnityScript; these terms (i.e., function and method) differ in at least two ways: in C# you need to specify the type of the data returned by this method, and the keyword **function** is not used anymore in C# for this purpose. We will see more about this topic in the next sections.

- Marking a block of instructions to be executed based on a condition: the keywords are **if…else**.

- Exiting a function: the keyword is **return**.

COMMENTS

In C# (similarly to JavaScript), you can use comments to explain the code and to make it more readable. This becomes important as the size of your code increases; and it is also important if you work as part of a team, so that team members can understand your code and make amendments in the right places, if and when it is needed.

When code is commented, it is not executed. There are two ways to comment your code in C#; you can use **single** or **multi-line** comments. In single-line comments, a **double forward slash** is added at the start of a line or after a statement, so that this line (or part thereof) is commented, as illustrated in the next code snippet.

```
//the next line prints Hello in the console window
print ("Hello");
//the next line declares the variable name
string name;
name = "Hello";//sets the value of the variable name
```

In multi-line comments, any text between /* and */ will be commented (and not executed). This is also refereed as **comment blocks**.

```
/* the next lines after the comments print hello in the console window
we then declare the variable name and assign a value
*/
print("Hello");
string name;
name = "Hello";//sets the value of the variable name
//print ("Hello World")
/*
    string name;
    name = "My Name";

*/
```

In addition to providing explanations about your code, you can also use comments to prevent part of your code to be executed. This is very useful when you would like to debug your code and find where the error or bug might be, using a very simple method. By commenting sections of your code, and using a process of elimination, you can usually find the issue quickly. For example, you can comment all the code and run the script; then comment half the code, and run the script. If it works, it means that the error is within the code that has been commented, and if it does not work, it means that the error is in the code that has not been commented. In the first case (if the code works), we could then just comment half of the portion of the code that has already been commented. So, by successively commenting more specific areas of our code, we can get to discover what part of the code includes the bug. This process is often called **dichotomy** (as we successively divide a code section into two). It is usually effective to debug your code because the number of iterations (dividing part of the code in two) is more predictable and also potentially less time-consuming. For example, for 100 lines of codes, we can successively narrow down the issue to 50, 25, 12, 6, and 3 lines (5 to 6 iterations in this case would be necessary instead of going through the whole 100 lines).

VARIABLES

A variable is a container. It includes a value that may change overtime. When using variables, we usually need to: (1) declare the variable (by specifying its type), (2) assign a value to this variable, and (3) possibly combine this variable with other variables using operators.

```
int myAge;//we declare the variable
myAge = 20;// we set the variable to 20
myAge = myAge + 1; //we add 1 to the variable myAge
```

In the previous example, we have declared a variable **myAge**, its type is **int** (integer), we set it to **20** and we then add 1 to it.

> Note that, contrary to UnityScript where the keyword **var** is used to declare a variable, in C# the variable is declared using its type followed by its name. As we will see later we will also need to use what is called an **access modifier** in order to specify how this variable can be accessed.

> Note that in the previous code we have assigned the value **myAge + 1** to **myAge**; the = operator is an assignment operator; in other words, it is there to assign a value to a variable and is not to be understood in a strict algebraic sense (i.e., that the values or variables on both sides of the = sign are equal).

Contrary to UnityScript, and to make coding easier and leaner, in C# you can perform a multiple declaration of several variables of the same type in the same statement. For example, in the next code snippet, we declare three variables, **v1**, **v2**, and **v3** in one statement. This is because they are of the same type (i.e., **integers**).

```
int v1,v2,v3;
int v4=4, v5=5, v6=6;
```

In the code above, the first line declares the variables v1, v2, and v3. All three are integers. In the second line, not only do we declare three variables simultaneously, but we also initialize them (i.e., set a value).

When using variables, there are a few things that we need to determine including their name, type and scope:

- **Name of a variable:** A variable is usually given a unique name so that it can be identified uniquely. The name of a variable is usually referred to as an identifier. When defining an identifier, it can contain letters, digits, a minus, an underscore or a dollar sign, and it usually begins with a letter. Identifiers cannot be keywords (e.g., such as **if**).

- **Type of variable:** variables can hold several types of data including numbers (e.g., **integers, doubles** or **floats**), text (i.e., strings or characters), Boolean values (e.g., true or false), arrays, objects (i.e., we will see this concept later in this chapter) or **GameObjects** (i.e., any object included in your scene), as illustrated in the next code snippet.

```
string myName = "Patrick";//the text is declared using double quotes
int currentYear = 2015;//the year needs no decimals and is declared as an integer
float width = 100.45f;//width is declared as a float (i.e., with decimals)
```

- **Variable declaration:** a variable needs to be declared so that the system knows what you referring to if you use it in your code. To create a variable, it needs to be declared. At the declaration stage, the variable does not have to be assigned a value, and this can be done later.

```
string myName;
myName = "My Name"
```

In the previous example, we declare a variable called **myName** and then assign the value **"My Name"** to it.

- **Scope of a variable:** a variable can be accessed (i.e., referred to) in specific contexts that depend on where in the script the variable was declared. We will look at this principle later.

- **Accessibility level:** as we will see later, a C# program consists of classes; for each of these classes, the methods and variables within can be accessed depending on **accessibility** levels. We will look at this principle later on (there is no need for any confusion at this stage :-)).

Common variable types include:

- **String**: same as text.
- **Int**: integer (1, 2, 3, etc.).
- **Boolean**: true or false.
- **Float**: with a fractional value (e.g., 1.2f, 3.4f, etc.).
- **Arrays**: a group of variables of the same type. If this is unclear, not to worry, this concept will be explained further in this chapter.
- **GameObject**: a game object (any game object in your scene).

ARRAYS

Sometimes, to make your code leaner, arrays make it easier to apply features and similar behaviors to a wide range of data. Arrays can help to declare less variables (for variables storing the same type of information) and to also access them more easily. When creating arrays, you can create single-dimensional arrays and multidimensional arrays.

Let's look at the simplest form of arrays: single-dimensional arrays. For this concept, we can take the analogy of a group of 10 people who all have a name. If we wanted to store this information using a string variable, we would need to declare (and set) ten different variables.

```
string name1;string name2; ......
```

While this code is perfectly fine, it would be great to store these in only one variable. For this purpose, we could use an array. An array is comparable to a list of elements that we access using an index. This index usually starts at 0 (for the first element in the list).

So let's see how we could do this with an array; first we could declare the array as follows:

```
string [] names;
```

You will probably notice the syntax **dataType [] nameofTheArray**. The **[]** syntax means that we declare an **array** of string values.

Then we could initialize the array, as we would normally do with any variable:

```
names = new string [10];
```

In the previous code, we just say that our new array called **names** will include 10 string variables.

We can then store information in this array as described in the next code snippet.

```
names [0] = "Paul";
names [1] = "Mary";
...
names [9] = "Pat";
```

In the previous code, we store the name **Paul** as the first element in the array (remember the index starts at 0); we store the second element (with the index 1) as **Mary**, as well as the last element (index is 9), **Pat**.

Introduction to Programming in C#

> Note that for an array of size **n**, **the index of the first element is 0** and **the index of the last element is n-1**. So for an array of size 10, the index for the first element is 0, and the index of the last element is 9.

If you were to use arrays of integers or floats, or any other type of data, the process would be similar.

Now, one of the cool things you can do with arrays is that you can initialize your array in one line, saving you the headaches of writing 10 lines of code if you have 10 variables, as illustrated in the next example.

```
string [] names = new string [10] {"Paul","Mary","John","Mark",
"Eva","Pat","Sinead","Elma","Flaithri", "Eleanor"};
```

This is very handy, as you will see in the next chapters, and this should definitely save you time coding.

Now that we have looked into single-dimensional arrays, let's look at multidimensional arrays, which can also be very handy when storing information. This type of array (i.e., multidimensional array) can be compared to a building with several floors, and on each floor, several apartments. So let's say that we would like to store the number of tenants for each apartment; we would, in this case, create variables that would store this number for each of these apartments.

The first solution would be to create variables that store the number of tenants for each of these apartments with a variable that makes reference to the floor, and the number of the apartment. For example **ap0_1** could be for the first apartment on the ground floor, **ap0_2**, would then be for the second apartment on the ground floor, **ap1_1**, would then be for the first apartment on the first floor, and **ap1_2**, would then be for the second apartment on the first floor. So in term of coding, we could have the following:

```
int ap0_1 = 0;
int ap0_2 = 0;
...
```

Using arrays instead we could do the following:

```
int [,] apArray = new int [10,10];
apArray [0,1] = 0;
apArray [0,2] = 0;
print (apArray[0]);
```

In the previous code:

- We declare our array. **int [,]** means an array that has two dimensions; in other words, we say that any element in this array will be defined and accessed based on two parameters: the floor level and the number of this apartment on that level.

[28]

- We also specify a size (or maximum) for each of these parameters. The maximum number of floors (level) will be 10, and the maximum number of apartment per floor will be 10. So, for this example we can define levels, from level 0 to level 9 (that would be 10 levels), and from apartment 0 to apartment 9 (that would be 10 apartment).

- The last line of code prints (in the **Console** window) the value of the first element of the array.

> One of the other interesting things with arrays is that, using a loop, you can write a single line of code to access all the elements of this array, and hence, write more efficient code.

CONSTANTS

So far we have looked at variables and how you can store and access them seamlessly. The assumption then was that a value may change over time, and that this value would be stored in a variable. However, there may be times when you know that a value will remain constant. For example, you may want to define labels that refer to values that should not change over time, and in this case, you could use constants. Let me explain: let's say that the player may have three choices in the game (e.g., referred to as 0, 1, and 2) and that you don't really want to remember these values, or that you would like to use a way that makes it easier to refer to them. Let's look at the following code:

```
int userChoice = 2;
if (userChoice == 0) print ("you have decided to restart");
if (userChoice == 1) print ("you have decided to stop the game");
if (userChoice == 2) print ("you have decided to pause the game");
```

In the previous code:

- The variable **userChoice** is an integer and is set to 1.
- Then we check its value and print a message accordingly.

Now, you may or may not remember that 0 corresponds to restarting the game; the same applies to the other two values. So instead, we could use constants to make it easier to remember (and use) these values. Let's look at the equivalent code that uses constants.

```
const int CHOICE_RESTART = 0;
const int CHOICE_STOP = 1;
const int CHOICE_PAUSE = 2;
int userChoice = 2;
if (userChoice == CHOICE_RESTART) print ("you have decided to restart");
if (userChoice == CHOICE_STOP) print ("you have decided to stop the game");
if (userChoice == CHOICE_PAUSE) print ("you have decided to pause the game");
```

In the previous code:

- We declare three **constant** variables.
- These variables are then used to check the choice made by the user.

In the next example, we use a constant to calculate a tax rate; this is a good practice as the same value will be used across the program with no or little room for errors when it comes to using the exact same tax rate across the code.

```
const float VAT_RATE = 0.21f;
float priceBeforeVat = 23.0f
float priceAfterVat = pricebeforeVat * VAT_RATE;
```

In the previous code:

- We declare a **constant** float variable for the vat rate.

- We declare a **float** variable for the item's price before the vat.

- We calculate the item's price after adding tax.

> It is a very good coding practice to use constants for values that don't change across your program. Using constants makes your code more readable; it saves work when you need to change a value in your code, and it also decreases possible occurrences of errors (e.g., for calculations).

OPERATORS

Once we have declared and assigned values to a variable, we can use operators to modify or combine variables. There are different types of operators including: arithmetic operators, assignment operators, comparison operators and logical operators.

Arithmetic operators are used to perform arithmetic operations including additions, subtractions, multiplications, or divisions. Common arithmetic operators include +, -, *, /, or % (modulo).

```
int number1 = 1;// the variable number1 is declared
int number2 = 1;// the variable number2 is declared
int sum = number1 + number2;// adding two numbers and store them in sum
int sub = number1 - number2;// subtracting two numbers and store them in sub
```

Assignment operators can be used to assign a value to a variable and include =, +=, -=, *=, /= or %=.

```
int number1 = 1;
int number2 = 1;
number1+=1; //same as number1 = number1 + 1;
number1-=1; //same as number1 = number1 - 1;
number1*=1; //same as number1 = number1 * 1;
number1/=1; //same as number1 = number1 / 1;
number1%=1; //same as number1 = number1 % 1;
```

> Note that the = operator, when used with strings, will concatenate strings (i.e., add them one after the other to create a new string). When used with a number and a string, the same will apply (for example **"Hello"+1** will result in **"Hello1"**).

Comparison operators are often used for conditions to compare two values; comparison operators include ==, !=, >, <, >= and >=.

```
if (number1 == number2); //if number1 equals number2
if (number1 != number2); //if number1 and number2 have different values
if (number1 > number2); //if number1 is greater than number2
if (number1 >= number2); //if number1 is greater than or equal to number2
if (number1 < number2); //if number1 is less than number2
if (number1 <= number2); //if number1 is less than or equal to number2
```

CONDITIONAL STATEMENTS

Statements can be performed based on a condition, and in this case they are called **conditional statements**. The syntax is usually as follows:

```
If (condition) statement;
```

This means **if the condition is verified (or true) then (and only then) the statement is executed**. When we assess a condition, we test whether a declaration is true. For example by typing **if (a == b)**, we mean **"if it is true that a equals to b"**. Similarly, if we type **if (a>=b)** we mean **"if its is true that a is greater than or equal to b"**

As we will see later on, we can also combine conditions. For example, we can decide to perform a statement if two (or more) conditions are true. For example, by typing **if (a == b && c == 2)** we mean **"if a equals to b and c equals to 2"**. In this case using the operator **&&** means **AND**, and that both conditions will need to be true. We could compare this to making a decision on whether we will go sailing tomorrow. For example **"if the weather is sunny and the wind speed is less than 5km/h then I will go sailing"**. We could translate this statement as follows.

```
if (weatherIsSunny == true && windSpeed < 5) IGoSailing = true;
```

When creating conditions, as for most natural languages, we can use the operator **OR** noted **||**. Taking the previous example, we could translate the following sentence **"if the weather is too hot or the wind is faster than 5km/h then I will not go sailing "** as follows.

```
if (weatherIsTooHot == true || windSpeed >5) IGoSailing = false;
```

Another example could be as follows.

```
if (myName == "Patrick") print("Hello Patrick");
else print ("Hello Stranger");
```

> When we deal with combining true or false statements, we are effectively applying what is called **Boolean logic**. Boolean logic deals with Boolean variables that have two values 1 and 0 (or true and false). By evaluating conditions, we are effectively processing Boolean numbers and applying Boolean logic. While you don't need to know about Boolean logic in depth, some operators for Boolean logic are important, including the **!** operator. It means **NOT** or the opposite. This means that if a variable is true, its opposite will be false, and vice versa. For example, if we consider the variable **weatherIsGood = true**, the value of **!weatherIsGood** will be **false** (its opposite). So the condition **if (weatherIdGood == false)** could be also written **if (!weatherIsGood)** which would literally translate as "if the weather is **NOT** good".

SWITCH STATEMENTS

If you have understood the concept of conditional statements, then this section should be pretty much straight forward. Switch statements are a variation on the if/else statements that we have seen earlier. The idea behind the switch statement is that, depending on the value of a particular variable, we will switch to a particular portion of the code and perform one or several actions. The variable considered for the switch structure is usually of type **integer**. Let's look at a simple example:

```
int choice = 1;
switch (choice)
{
    case 1:
        print ("you chose 1");
        break;
    case 2:
        print ("you chose 2");
        break;
    case 3:
        print ("you chose 3");
        break;
    default:
        print ("Default option");
        break;
}
print ("We have exited the switch structure");
```

In the previous code:

- We declare the variable **choice**, as an **integer** and initialize it to **1**.

- We then create a **switch** structure whereby, depending on the value of the variable **choice**, the program will switch to the relevant section (i.e., the portion of code starting with **case 1:**, **case 2:**, etc.). Note that in our code, we look for the values 1, 2 or 3. However, if the variable **choice** does not equal 1 or 2 or 3, the program will branch to the section called **default**. This is because this section is executed if any of the other possible choices (i.e., 1,2, or 3) have not been fulfilled (or selected).

> Note that each choice or branch starts with the keyword **case** and ends with **break**. The **break** statement is there to specify that after executing the commands included in the branch (or current choice), it should exit the switch structure. Without any break statement the next line of code will be executed.

So let's consider the previous example and see how this would work. In our case, the variable **choice** is set to **1**, so we will enter the **switch** structure, and then look for the section that deals with a value of **1** for the variable **choice**. This will be the section that starts with **case 1:**; then the command **print ("you chose 1");** will be executed, followed by the command **break**, indicating that we should exit the switch structure; finally the command **print ("We have exited the switch structure")** will be executed.

> Switch structures are very useful to structure your code and when dealing with mutually exclusive choices (i.e., only one of the choices can be processed) based on an integer value, especially in the case of menus. In addition switch structures make for cleaner and easily understandable code.

Loops

There are times when you have to perform repetitive tasks as a programmer; many times, these can be fast forwarded using loops. Loops are structures that will perform the same actions repetitively based on a condition. So, the process is usually as follows:

- Start the loop.
- Perform actions.
- Check for a condition.
- Exit the loop if the condition is fulfilled or keep looping.

Sometimes the condition is performed at the start of the loop, some other times it is performed at the end of the loop.

Let's take the following example that is using a **while** loop.

```
int counter =0;
while (counter <=10)
{
    print ("Counter = " + counter);
    counter++;
}
```

In the previous code:

- We set the value of the variable **counter**.
- We then create a loop that is delimited by the curly brackets and that starts with the keyword **while**.
- We set the condition to remain in this loop (i.e., **counter <=10**).
- Within the loop, we increase the value of the variable **counter** by 1 and print its value.

So effectively:

- The first time we go through the loop: the variable **counter** is increased to **1**; we reach the end of the loop; we go back to the start of the loop and check if **counter** is <=10; this is true in this case (**counter** = 1).
- The second time we go through the loop: **counter** is increased to 2; we reach the end of the loop; we go back to the start of the loop and check if **counter** is <=10; this is true in this case (**counter** = 2).

- ...

    - The 11th time we go through the loop: **counter** is increased to 11; we reach the end of the loop; we go back to the start and check if **counter** is <=10; this is now false in this case (**counter** = 11). As a result, we then exit the loop.

So, as you can see, using a loop, we have managed to increment the value of the variable **counter** iteratively, from 0 to 11, but using less code than would be needed otherwise.

Now, we could create a slightly modified version of this loop; let's look at the following example:

```
int counter =0;
do
{
    print ("Counter = " + counter);
    counter++;
} while (counter <=10);
```

In this example, you may spot two differences, compared to the previous code:

- The **while** keyword is now at the end of the loop. So the condition will be evaluated (or assessed) at the end of the loop.

- A **do** keyword is now featured at the start of the loop.

- In this example, we perform statements and then check for the condition.

Another variations of the code could be as follows:

```
for (int counter = 0; counter <=10; counter ++)
{
    print ("Counter = " + counter);
}
```

In the previous code:

- We declare a loop in a slight different way: we say that we will use an integer variable called **counter** that will go from 0 to 10.

- This variable **counter** will be incremented by 1 every time we go through the loop.

- We remain in the loop as long as the variable **counter** is less than or equal to 10.

- The test for the condition, in this case, is performed at the start of the loop.

> Loops are very useful to be able to perform repetitive actions for a finite number of objects, or to perform what is usually referred as recursive actions. For example, you could use loops to create (i.e., instantiate) 100 objects at different locations (this will save you some code :-)), or to go through an array of 100+ elements.

CLASSES

When coding in C# with Unity, you will be creating scripts that are either classes or use built-in classes. So what is a class?

As we have seen earlier, C# is an object-oriented programming (OOP) language. Put simply, a C# program will consist of a collection of objects that interact amongst themselves. Each object has one or more attributes, and it is possible to perform actions on these objects using what are called **methods**. In addition, objects that share the same properties are said to belong to the same **class**. For example, we could take the analogy of a bike. There are bikes of all shapes and colors; however, they share common features. For example they all have a specific number of wheels (e.g., one, two or three) or a speed; they can have a color, and actions can be performed on these bikes (e.g., accelerate, turn right, turn left, etc.). So in object-oriented programming, the class would be **bike**, speed or color would be referred as member variables, and accelerate (i.e., an action) would be referred as member methods. So if we were to define a common type, we could define a class called **Bike** and for this class define several member variables and attributes that would make it possible to define and perform actions on the objects of type **Bike**.

This is, obviously, a simplified explanation of classes and objects, but it should give you a clearer idea of the concept of object-oriented programming, if you are new to it.

DEFINING A CLASS

So now that we have a clearer idea of what a class is, let's see how we could define a class. So let's look at the following example.

```
public class Bike
{
    private float speed;
    private int color;

    private void accelerate()
    {
        speed++;
    }
    private void turnRight()
    {
    }
}
```

In the code above, we have defined a class, called **Bike**, that includes two member variables (**speed** and **color**) as well as two member methods (**accelerate** and **turnRight**). Let's look at the script a little closer; you may notice a few things:

- The name of the class is preceded by the keywords **public class**; in OOP terms, the keyword **public** is called an **access modifier** and it defines how (and from where) this class may be accessed and used. In C# there are at least five types of access modifiers, including **public** (no restricted access), **protected** (access limited to the containing class or types derived from this class), **internal** (access is limited to the current assembly), **protected internal** (we won't be using this access mode in this book), and **private** (access only from the containing type).

- The names of all variables are preceded by their type (i.e., int), and the keyword **private**: this means that these integer variables will be accessible only for objects of types **Bike**.

- The name of each method is preceded by the keywords **private void**: the **void** keyword means that the method does not return any data back, while the keyword **private** means that the method will be accessible only from the containing type (i.e., **Bike**). In other word, only objects of type **Bike** will be able to access this method.

ACCESSING CLASS MEMBERS AND VARIABLES

Once a class has been defined, it's great to be able to access its member variables and methods. In C# (as for other object-oriented programming languages), this can be done using the **dot notation**.

> The dot notation refers to **object-oriented programming**. Using dots, you can access properties and functions (or methods) related to a particular object. For example **gameObject.transform.position** gives you access to the **position** from the **transform** of the object linked to this script. It is often useful to read it backward; in this case, the dot can be interpreted as "**of**". So in our case, **gameObject.transform.position** can be translated as "the position **of** the transform **of** the **gameObject**".

Once a class has been defined, objects based on this class can be created. For example, if we were to create a new **Bike** object, based on the code that we have seen above, the following code could be used.

```
Bike myBike = new Bike();
```

This code will create an object based on the "template" **Bike**. You may notice the syntax:

```
dataType variable = new dataType()
```

By default, this new object will include all the member variables and methods defined earlier. So it will have a color and a speed, and we should also be able to access its **accelerate** and **turnRight** methods. So how can this be done? Let's look at the next code snippet that shows how we can access these.

```
Bike b = new Bike();
b.speed = 12.3f
b.color = 2;
b.accelerate();
```

In the previous code:

- The new bike **myBike** is created.
- Its speed is set to **12.3** and its color to **2**.
- The speed is then increased after calling the **accelerate** method.
- Note that to assign an object's attribute or method we use the dot notation.

Introduction to Programming in C#

> When defining member variables and methods, it is usually good practice to restrict the access to member variables (e.g., private type) and to define public methods with no or less strict restrictions (e.g., public) that provide access to these variables. These methods are often referred to as **getters** and **setters** (because you can get or set values from them).

To illustrate this concept, let's look at the following code:

```
public class Bike
{
    private float speed;
    private int color;

    private void accelerate()
    {
        speed++;
    }
    public void setSpeed (float newSpeed)
    {
        speed = newSpeed;
    }
    public float getSpeed ()
    {
        return (speed)
    }

    private void turnRight()
    {
    }
}
```

In the previous code, we have declared two new methods: **setSpeed** and **getSpeed**.

- For **setSpeed**: the type is **void** as this method does not return any information, and its access is set to **public**, so that it can be accessed with no restrictions.

- For **getSpeed**: the type is **float** as this method returns the speed, which type is float. Its access is set to **public**, so that it can be accessed with no restrictions.

So, we could combine the code created to date in one program (or new class) as follows in Unity.

```
using UnityEngine;
using System.Collections;

public class TestCode : MonoBehaviour {
    public class Bike
    {
        private float speed;
        private int color;

        private void accelerate()
        {
            speed++;
        }
        public void setSpeed (float newSpeed)
        {
            speed = newSpeed;
        }
        public float getSpeed ()
        {
            return (speed);
        }

        private void turnRight()
        {
        }
    }
    public void Start ()
    {
        Bike myBike = new Bike();
        myBike.setSpeed (23.0f);
        print (myBike.getSpeed());
    }
}
```

In the previous code, you may notice at least two differences compared to the previous code that we have created:

- At the start of the code, the following two lines of code have been added:

```
using UnityEngine;
using System.Collections;
```

- The keyword **using** is called a directive; in this particular case it is used to import what is called a **namespace**; put simply, by adding this directive you are effectively importing (or gaining access to) a collection of classes or data types. Each of these namespaces or "libraries" includes useful classes for your program. For example, the namespace **UnityEngine** will include classes for Unity development and **System.Collections** will include classes and interfaces for different collections of objects. By default, whenever

Introduction to Programming in C#

you create a new C# script in Unity, these two namespaces (and associated directives) are included.

- We have declared our class **Bike** within another class called **TestCode**. **TestCode** is, in this case, the containing class.

```
public class TestCode : MonoBehaviour {
```

- Whenever you create a new C# script, the name of the script (for example **TestCode** will be used to define the main class within the script; i.e., **TestCode**).

- The **syntax : Monobehavior** means that the class **TestCode** is derived from the class **MonoBehaviour**. This is often referred to as inheritance.

CONSTRUCTORS

As we have seen in the previous section, when a new object is created, it will, by default, include all the member variables and methods. To create this object, we would use the name of the class, followed by (), as per the next example.

```
Bike myBike = new Bike();
myBike.color = 2;
myBike.speed = 12.3f;
```

In fact, it is possible to change some of the properties of the new object created at the time it is initialized. For example, instead of setting the speed and the color of the object as we have done in the previous code, it would be great to be able to set these automatically and pass the parameter accordingly when the object is created. Well, this can be done with what is called a **constructor**. A constructor literally helps to construct your new object based on parameters (also referred as arguments) and instructions. So, for example, let's say that we would like the color of our bike to be specified when it is created; we could modify the **Bike** class, as follows, by adding the following method:

```
public Bike (int newColor)
{
    color = newColor;
}
```

This is a new constructor (the name of the method is the same as the class), and it takes an integer as a parameter; so after modifying the description of our class (as per the code above), we could then create a new bike object as follows:

```
Bike myBike = new Bike(2);
//myBike.color = 2;
myBike.speed = 12.3f;
```

We could even specify a second constructor that would include both the color and the speed as follows:

```
public Bike (int newColor, float newSpeed)
{
    color = newColor;
    speed = newSpeed;
}
```

You can have different constructors in your class; the constructor used at the initialization stage will be the one that matches the arguments passed.

For example, let's say that we have two constructors for our Bike class.

```
public Bike (int newColor, float newSpeed)
{
        color = newColor;
        speed = newSpeed;
}
public Bike (int newColor)
{
        color = newColor;
}
```

If a new **Bike** object is created as follows:

```
Bike newBike = new Bike (2)
```

...then the first constructor will be called.

If a new **Bike** object is created as follows:

```
Bike newBike = new Bike (2, 10.0f)
```

...then the second constructor will be called.

You may also wonder what happens if the following code is used since no default constructor has been defined.

```
Bike newBike = new Bike ();
```

In fact, whenever you create your class, a default constructor is also defined (implicitly) and evoked whenever a new object is created using the **new** operator with no arguments. This is called a default constructor. In this case, the default values for each of the types of the numerical member variables are used (e.g., 0 for integers or false for Boolean variables).

> Note that access to constructors is usually public, except in the particular cases where we would like a class not to be instantiated (e.g., for classes that include **static** members only). Also note that, as for variables, if no access modifiers are specified, these will be **private** by default. This is similar for methods.

DESTRUCTORS

As for constructors, when an object is deleted, the corresponding destructor is called. Its name is the same as the class and preceded by a tilde ~; as illustrated in the next code snippet.

```
~Bike()
{
        print("Object has been destroyed");
}
```

This being said, a destructor can neither take parameters (or arguments) nor return a value.

STATIC MEMBERS OF A CLASS

When a method or variable is declared as static, only one instance of this member exists for a class. So a static variable will be "shared" between instances of this class. Static variables are usually used to retrieve constants without instantiating a class. The same applies for static method: they can be evoked without having to instantiate a class. This can be very useful if you want to create and avail of tools. For example, in Unity, it is possible to use the method **GameObject.Find**(); this method usually makes it possible to look for a particular object based on its name. Let's look at the following example.

```
public void Start()
{
      GameObject t = (GameObject) GameObject.Find("test");
}
```

In the previous code, we look for an object called test, and store the result inside the variable **t** of type **GameObject**. However, when we use the syntax **GameObject.Find**, we use the static method **Find** that is available from the class **GameObject**. There are many other static functions that you will be able to use in Unity, including **Instantiate**. Again, these functions can be called without the need to instantiate an object. The following code snippet provides another example based on the class **Bike**.

```
using UnityEngine;
using System.Collections;

public class TestCode : MonoBehaviour {

    public class Bike
    {
        private float speed;
        private int color;
        private static nbBikes;
        private int countBikes()
        {
            nbBikes++;
        }
        private int getNbBikes()
        {
            return(nbBikes);
        }
    }
    public void Start ()
    {
        Bike bike1 = new Bike();
        Bike bike2 = new Bike();
        bike1.countBikes();
        bike2.countBikes();
        print("Nb Bikes:"+getNbBikes());

    }
}
```

The following code illustrates the use of static functions.

```
using UnityEngine;
using System.Collections;

public class TestCode : MonoBehaviour {

    public class Bike
    {
        private float speed;
        private int color;
        public static sayHello()
        {
            print ("Hello");
        }
    }
    public void Start ()
    {
        Bike.sayHello();
    }
}
```

The previous code would result in the following output:

```
Hello
```

In the previous code, we declare a static method called **sayHello**; this method is then called in the start method without the need to instantiate (or create) a new **Bike**. This is because, due to its **public** and **static** attributes, it can be accessed from anywhere in the program.

INHERITANCE

I hope everything is clear so far, as we are going to look at a very interesting and important principle for object-oriented programming: inheritance. The main idea of inheritance is that objects can inherit their properties from other objects (their parent). As they inherit these properties, they can remain identical or evolve and overwrite some of these inherited properties. This is very interesting because it makes it possible to minimize the code by creating a class with general properties for all objects sharing similar features, and then, if need be, to overwrite and customize some of these properties.

Let's take the example of vehicles; they would generally have the following properties:

- Number of wheels.
- Speed.
- Number of passengers.
- Color.
- Capacity to accelerate.
- Capacity to stop.

So we could create the following class for example:

```
class Vehicles
{
    private int nbWheels;
    private float speed;
    private int nbPassengers;
    private int color;
    private void accelerate()
    {
        speed++;
    }
}
```

These features could apply for example to cars, bikes, motorbikes, or trucks. However, all these vehicles also differ; some of them may or may not have an engine or a steering wheel. So we could create a subclass called **MotorizedVehicles**, based on **Vehicles**, but with specificities linked to the fact that they are motorized. These added attributes could be:

- Engine size.
- Petrol type.

- Petrol levels.
- Ability to fill-up the tank.

The following example illustrates how this class could be created.

```
class MotoredVehicles: Vehicles
{
        private float engineSize;
        private int petrolType;
        private float petrolLevels;
        private void fillUpTank()
        {
                petrolLevels+=10;
        }
}
```

- When the class is defined, its name is followed by : **Vehicles**. This means that it inherits from the class **Vehicles**. So it will, by default, avail of all the methods and variables already included in the class **Vehicles**.

- We have created a new member method for this class, called **fillUpTank**.

- In the previous example, you may notice that the methods and variables that were defined for the class **Vehicles** do not appear here; this is because they are implicitly added to this new class, since it inherits from the class **Vehicles**.

Whenever you create a new class in Unity, it will, by default, inherit from the **MonoBehaviour** class; as a result it will implicitly include all the member methods and variables of the class **MonoBehaviour**. Some of these methods include **Start** or **Update**, for example.

> When using inheritance, the parent is usually referred to as the **base class**, while the child is referred to as the **inherited class**.

Now, while the child inherits "Behaviors" from its parents, these can always be modified or, put simply, overwritten. However, in this case, the base method (the method defined in the parent) must be declared as virtual. Also, when overriding this method, the keyword **override** must be used. This is illustrated in the following code.

```
class Vehicles
{
        private int nbWheels;
        private float speed;
        private int nbPassengers;
        private int color;
        private virtual void accelerate()
        {
                speed++;
        }
}
class MotoredVehicles: Vehicles
{
        private float engineSize;
        private int petrolType;
        private float petrolLevels;
        private void fillUpTank()
        {
                petrolLevels+=10;
        }
        private override void accelerate()
        {
                speed+=10;
        }
}
```

In the previous example, while the method **accelerate** is inherited from the class **Vehicles**, it would normally increase the speed by one. However, by overwriting it, we make sure that in the case of objects instantiated from the class **MotoredVehicles**, each acceleration increases the speed by 10.

This point can also be illustrated using some classes in Unity. Let's look at the next example.

Introduction to Programming in C#

```
using UnityEngine;
using System.Collections;

public class TestCode : MonoBehaviour {

    public class Bike
    {
        private float speed;
        private int color;
        public static sayHello()
        {
            print ("Hello");
        }
    }
    public void Start ()
    {
        Bike.sayHello();
    }
}
```

In this example, we have created a class **TestCode**; this class inherits from **MonoBehaviour**; by default this class includes, amongst other things, a definition for the methods **Start** and **Update**; however, by default, these two methods are blank; this is the reason why we overwrite these methods for the class **TestCode** (inherited from **MonoBehaviour**) so that the **Start** method actually displays some information.

There are obviously more concepts linked to inheritance; however, the information provided in this section should get you started easily. For more information on inheritance in C#, you can **look at the official documentation**.

METHODS

Methods or functions can be compared to a friend or colleague to whom you gently ask to perform a task, based on specific instructions, and to return the information to you then. For example, you could ask your friend the following: "**Can you please tell me when I will be celebrating my 20th birthday given that I was born in 2000**". So you give your friend (who is good at Math :-)) the information (date of birth) and s/he will calculate the year of your 20th birthday and give this information back to you. So in other words, your friend will be given an input (i.e., the date of birth) and return an output (i.e., the year of your 20th birthday). Methods work exactly this way: they are given information (and sometimes not), perform an action, and then (sometimes, if needed) return information back.

In programming terms, a method (or function) is a block of instructions that performs a set of actions. It is executed when invoked (or put more simply **called**) from the script, or when an event occurs (e.g., the player has clicked on a button or the player collides with an object; we will see more about events in the next section). As for member variables, member functions or methods are declared and they can also be called.

Methods are very useful because once the code for a method has been created, it can be called several times without the need to re-write the same code over and over again. Also, because methods can take parameters, a method can process these parameters and produce or return information accordingly; in other words, they can perform different actions and produce different information based on the input. As a result, methods can do one or all of the following:

- Perform an action.

- Return a result.

- Take parameters and process them.

A method has a syntax and can be declared as follows (in at least two ways).

```
AccessType typeOfdataReturned nameOfTheFunction ()
{
        Perform actions here...
}
```

In the previous code the method does not take any input; neither does it return an output. It just performs actions.

OR

```
AccessType typeOfDataReturned nameOfTheFunction ()
{
        Perform actions here...
}
```

Let's look at the following method for instance.

```
public int calculateSum(int a, int b)
{
        return (a+b);
}
```

In the previous code:

- The method is of type **public**: there are no access restrictions.

- The method will return an integer.

- The name of the method is **calculateSum**.

- The method takes two arguments (i.e., integer parameters).

- The method returns the sum of the two parameters passed (the parameters are referred to as **a** and **b** within this method).

A method can be called using the () operator, as follows:

```
nameOfTheFunction1();
nameOfTheFunction2(value);
int test = nameOfTheFunction3(value);
```

In the previous code, a method is called with no parameter (line 1), or with a parameter (line 2). In the third example (line 3), a variable called **test** will be set with the value returned by the method **nameOfTheFunction3**.

> You may, and we will get to this later, have different methods in a class with the exact same name but that take different types of parameters. This is often referred as polymorphism, as the method literally takes different forms and can process information differently based on the information (e.g., type of data) provided.

ACCESSING METHODS AND ACCESS MODIFIERS

As we have seen previously, in C# there are different types of access modifiers. These modifiers specify from where a method can be called and can be **public** (no restricted access), **protected** (access is limited to the containing class or types derived from this class), **internal** (access is limited to the current assembly), **protected internal** (we won't use this access type in this book), and **private** (i.e., access is limited to the containing type).

COMMON METHODS

In Unity, there are many methods available by default, and they are called built-in methods. Some of these functions are called when an event occurs. For example:

- **Start**: called at the start of the scene.

- **Update**: called every time the screen is refreshed.

- **OnControllerColliderHit**: called whenever the **First-Person Controller** (a built-in controller used to make it possible to navigate through your scene using a first-person view) collides with an object.

As we will see later, because most of your classes will inherit by default from the class **MonoBehaviour**, they will, by default, include several methods, including **Start** and **Update** that you will be able to override (i.e., modify for your own use).

SCOPE OF VARIABLES

Whenever you create a variable in C#, you will need to be aware of the scope and access type of the variable so that you use it where its scope makes it possible for you to do so.

The scope of a variable refers to where you can use this variable in a script. In C#, we usually make the difference between **global variables** and **local variables**.

> You can compare the term **local** and **global** variables to a language that is either local or global. In the first case, the local language will only be used (i.e., spoken) by the locals, whereas the global language will be used (i.e., spoken) and understood by anyone whether they are locals or part of the global community.

When you create a class definition along with member variables, these variables will be seen by any method within your class.

Global variables are variables that can be used anywhere in your script, hence the name global. These variables need to be declared at the start of the script (using the usual declaration syntax) and outside of any method; they can then be used anywhere in the script as illustrated in the next code snippet.

```
class MyBike
{
    private int color;
    private float speed;

    public void accelerate()
    {
        speed++;
    }
}
```

In the previous code we declare the variable **speed** as a global variable and access it from the method accelerate.

Local variables are declared within a method and are to be used only within this method, hence the term local, because they can only be used locally, as illustrated in the next code snippet.

Introduction to Programming in C#

```
public void Start()
{
    int myVar;
    myVar = 0;
}
public void Update()
{
    int myVar2;
    myVar2 = 2;
}
```

In the previous code, **myVar** is a local variable to the method **Start**, and can only be used within this function; **myVar2** is a local variable to the method **Update**, and can only be used within this method.

EVENTS

Throughout this book and in C#, you will read about and use events. So what are they?

Well, put simply, events can be compared to something that happens at a particular time, and when this event occurs, something (e.g., an action) needs to be done. If we make an analogy with daily activities: when the alarm goes off (event) we can either get-up (action) or decide to go back to sleep. When you receive an email (event), you can decide to read it (action), and then reply to the sender (another action).

In computer terms, it is quite similar, although the events that we will be dealing with will be slightly different. So, we could be waiting for the user to press a key (event) and then move the character accordingly (action), or wait until the user clicks on a button on screen (event) to load a new scene (action).

In Unity, whenever an event occurs, a function (or method) is usually called (the function, in this case, is often referred as a handler, because it "handles" the event). You have then the opportunity to modify this function and add instructions (i.e. statements) that should be followed, should this event occur.

> To take the analogy of daily activities: we could write instructions to a friend on a piece of paper, so that, in case someone calls in our absence, the friend knows exactly what to do. So an event handler is basically a set of instructions (usually stored within a function) to be followed in case a particular event occurs.

Sometimes information is passed to this method about the particular event, and sometimes not. For example, when the screen is refreshed the method **Update** is called. When the game starts (i.e., when a particular script is enabled), the method **Start** is called. When there is a collision between the player and an object, the method **OnControllerColliderHit** is called. In this particular case (i.e., collision), an object is usually passed to the method that handles the event so that we get to know more about the other object involved in the collision.

As you can see, there can be a wide range of events in our game, and we will get to that later on. In this book, we will essentially be dealing with the following events:

- **Start**: when a script is enabled (e.g., start of the scene).

- **Update**: when the screen is refreshed (e.g., every frame).

- **OnControllerColliderHit**: when a collision occurs between the player and another object.

- **Awake**: when the game starts (i.e., once).

POLYMORPHISM (GENERAL CONCEPTS)

The word polymorphism takes it's meaning from **poly** (several) and **morph** (shape); so it literally means several forms. In object-oriented programming, it refers to the ability to process objects differently (or more specifically) depending on their data type or class. Let's take the example of adding. If we want to add two numbers, we will make an algebraic addition (e.g., 1 + 2). However, adding two **string** variables may mean concatenating them (adding them one after the other). For example, adding the text "Hello" and the text "World" would result in the text "**HelloWorld**". As you can see, the way an operation is performed on different data types may vary and produce different results. So again, with polymorphism we will be able to customize methods (or operations) so that data is processed based on its type of class. So, let's look at the following code which illustrates how this can be done in C#.

```csharp
public class AddObjects
{
    public int add (int a, int b)
    {
        return (a + b);
    }
    public string add (string a, string b)
    {
        return (a + b);
    }
}
```

In the previous code, it is possible to add two different types of data: integers and strings. Depending on whether two integers or two strings are passed as parameters, we will be calling either the first **add** method or the second **add** method.

DYNAMIC POLYMORPHISM

In C#, dynamic polymorphism can be achieved using both abstract classes and virtual functions.

In C#, it is possible to create a class that will provide a partial implementation of an interface. Broadly, an interface defines what a class should include (i.e., member methods, member variables or events), but it does not declare how these should be implemented. So, an abstract class will include abstract methods or variables; which means that this class will define the name and type of the variables, the name of the methods, as well as the type of data returned by this method. It is called **abstract** because you cannot implement this type of class (it can never be "materialized"); however, it can be used as a template (or "dream" class) for derived classes. Let's look at the following example.

```
abstract class Vehicule
{
    public abstract void decelerate();
}

class Bike: Vehicule
{
    private float speed;
    private int color;
    public Bike (float newSpeed)
    {
        speed = newSpeed;
    }
    public override void decelerate()
    {
        speed --;
    }
}
```

In the previous code:

- We declare an abstract class **Vehicle**.
- We declare an abstract method called **decelerate**.
- We then create a new class called **Bike**, inherited from the abstract class **Vehicle**.
- We then override the abstract method **decelerate** to use our own implementation.

Introduction to Programming in C#

> Using an abstract class just means that we list methods that would be useful for the children; however, the children will have to define how the method should be implemented.

The second way to implement dynamic polymorphism is by using **virtual** methods or variables. In the case of **virtual methods**, we declare a method that will be used by default by objects of this class or inherited classes; however, in this case, even if the method is ready to be used (i.e., because we have defined how it should be implemented), it can be changed (or overridden) by the child (i.e., the inherited class) to fit a specific purpose. In this case (i.e., inherited method), we need to specify that we override this method using the keyword **override**.

> The key difference between an abstract and a virtual method is that, while an abstract method should be overridden, a virtual methods may be overridden if the base method (that is, the method declared in the base class) does not suit a particular purpose.

Let's look at an example:

```
class Vehicle
{
    private float speed;
    public virtual accelerate()
    {
        speed +=10;
    }
}

class Bike: Vehicle
{
    public override accelerate()
    {
        speed++;
    }
}
```

In the previous code:

- We declare a class **Vehicle**.

- It includes both a private variable **speed** and a virtual method called **accelerate**. This method is virtual, which means that inherited classes will be able to modify (override) it, if need be.

- We then create a new class **Bike** that inherits form the class **Vehicle**. In this class, we override the method accelerate using the keyword **override** so that the speed is just incremented by one.

WORKFLOW TO CREATE A SCRIPT

There are many ways to create and use scripts in Unity, but generally the process is as follows:

- Create a new script using the **Project** view (**Create | C# Script**) or the main menu (**Assets | Create | C# Script**).

- Attach the script to an object (e.g., drag and drop the script on the object).

- Check in the **Console** window that there are no errors in the script.

- Play the scene.

When you create your script, by default, the name of the class within the script will be the name of the script. So let's say that you created a new script called **TestCode**, then the following code will be automatically generated within:

```
using UnityEngine;
using System.Collections;

public class TestCode : MonoBehaviour
{
    public void Start ()
    {
    }
    public void Update ()
    {
    }
}
```

In the previous code, the class **TestCode** has been created; it inherits from the class **MonoBehaviour**, and it includes two methods that can be modified: **Start** and **Update**. You will also notice the two namespaces **UnityEngine** and **System.Collections**. As we have seen earlier, the keywords **using** is called a directive; in this particular case it is used to import what is called a namespace; put simply, by adding this directive you are effectively importing a collection of classes or data types. Each of these namespaces or "libraries" includes useful classes for your programme. For example the namespace **UnityEngine** will include classes for Unity development and **System.Collections** will include classes and interfaces, for different collections of objects. You can of course create classes that will not be linked to any object, and used to instantiate new objects.

How scripts are compiled

Whenever you create and save a script it is compiled and Unity will notify you (using the **Console** window) of any error. This being said, the order in which the scripts are compiled depends on its location. First, the scripts located in the folders **Standard Assets**, **Pro Standard Assets or Plugins**, then the scripts located in **Standard Assets/Editor**, **Pro Assets/Editor** or **Plugins/Editor**, and then the scripts outside the **Editor** folder, followed by the scripts in the **Editor** folder. For more information on script compilation, you can **check the official documentation**.

CODING CONVENTION

When you are coding, there are usually naming conventions based on the language that you are using. These often provide increased clarity for your code and depend on the language that you will be using.

Naming conventions usually employ a combination of camel casing and Pascal casing.

- In camel casing all words included in a name, except for the first one, is capitalized (e.g., myVariable).

- In Pascal casing all words included in a name are capitalized (e.g., MyVariable).

When coding in C# for example, naming conventions will use a combinations of camel an Pascal casing depending on whether you are naming a class, an interface, a variable or a resource.

However, as a C# beginner, in addition to learn about classes, methods, or inheritance, it may not be necessary to adhere completely to this naming convention at the start, at least as long as you use a consistent naming scheme.

So, while it is good to acknowledge different naming conventions for programming language and to understand why there are in place, and to keep things simple, this book will use a simplified naming convention, as follows:

- Classes (Pascal casing).

- All methods and variables (camel casing).

Once you feel comfortable with C# and want to know more about the official naming scheme, you may look at Microsoft **official naming guidelines**.

A FEW THINGS TO REMEMBER WHEN YOU CREATE A SCRIPT (CHECKLIST)

As you create your first scripts in the next chapter, there will be, without a doubt, errors and possibly hair pulling :-). You see, when you start coding, you will, as for any new activity, make small mistakes, learn what they are, improve your coding, and ultimately get better at writing your scripts. As I have seen students learning scripting, there are some common errors that are usually made; these don't make you a bad programmer; on the contrary, it is part of the learning process.

> We all learn by trial and error, and making mistakes is part of the learning process.

So, as you create your first script, set any fear aside, try to experiment, be curious, and get to learn the language. It is like learning a new foreign language: when someone from a foreign country understands your first sentences, you feel so empowered! So, it will be the same with C#, and to ease the learning process, I have included a few tips and things to keep in mind when writing your scripts, so that you progress even faster. You don't need to know all of these by now (I will refer to these later on, in the next chapter), but just be aware of it and also use this list if any error occurs (this list is also available as a pdf file in the resource pack, so that you can print it and keep it close by). So, watch out for these :-).

- Each opening bracket has a corresponding closing bracket.

- All variables are written consistently (e.g., spelling and case). The name of each variable is case-sensitive; this means that if you declare a variable **myvariable** but then refer to it as **myVariable** later on in the code, this may trigger an error, as the variable **myVariable** and **myvariable**, because they have a different case (upper- or lower-case **V**), are seen as two different variables.

- All variables are declared (type and name) prior to being used (e.g., **int**).

- The type of the argument passed to a method is the type that is required by this method.

- The type of the argument returned by a method is the type that is required to be returned by this method.

- Built-in functions are spelt with the proper case (e.g., upper-case **U** for **Update**).

- Use **camel casing** (i.e., capitalize the first character of each word except for the first word) or **Pascal casing** (i.e., capitalize the first character of each word) consistently.

- All statements are ended with a semi-colon.

- For **if** statements the condition is within round brackets.

- For **if** statements the condition uses the syntax "==" rather than "=".

- When calling a method, the exact name of this method (i.e., case-sensitive) is used.

- When referring to a variable, it is done with regards to the access type of the variable (e.g., public or private).

- Local variables are declared and can be used within the same method.

- Global variables are declared outside methods and can be used anywhere within the class.

LEVEL ROUNDUP

Summary

In this chapter, we have become familiar with C# and different programming concepts. We also looked into object-oriented programming. In the next chapter, we will harness these skills to be able to create (and execute) our first script.

Quiz

It is now time to test your knowledge. Please answer the following questions. The answers are available in the resource pack.

1. The following statement will print the text **Hello World** in the **Console** window.

```
print("Hello World");
```

2. The value of the variable **c** in the following statement will be **3**.

```
int a;
int b;
a = 1;
b =1;
c = a + b;
```

3. The value of the variable **fullName**, in the following code snippet, will be **JohnPaul**.

```
string fName = "John";
string lName = "Paul";
string fullName = fName + lName;
```

4. The following code snippet will print **I will not go sailing**.

```
bool windIsStrong;
windIsStrong = true;
if (windIsStrong) print ("I will not go sailing");
```

5. The following code snippet will print **I will not go sailing**.

```
bool weatherIsSunny;
bool windIsStrong;
bool iWillGoSailing;
weatherIsSunny = true;
windIsStrong = false;
If (weatherIsSunny && !windIsStrong ) print ("I will go sailing");
If (!weatherIsSunny || windIsStrong ) print ("I will not go sailing");
```

6. Spot three coding mistakes in the following snippet.

```
int test
int test2;
test3 = 0;
test 3 = test1 + test2;
```

7. Consider the method described in the next code snippet, and select the correct way to call it (i.e., A, B, or C):

a) **displayMessage();**
b) **displayAMessage()**
c) **displayAMessage();**

```
public void displayAMessage()
{
}
```

8. The value of the variable **counter** in the following code snippet will be **3** after the code has been executed.

```
int counter;
counter = 0;
counter = counter + 1;
```

9. The following code will print the message **Hello** every second.

```
public void Update()
{
    print ("Hello");
}
```

10. A local variable can be used from any part of a script.

Solutions to the Quiz

1. TRUE.

2. FALSE.

3. TRUE.

4. TRUE.

5. FALSE

6.
```
int test
int test2;
test3 = 0;//no type defined for test3
test 3 = test1 + test2;//test1 not declared yet
```

7. a) displayMessage();

8. FALSE.

9. FALSE (it will be displayed every frame).

10. FALSE (only where it was declared).

Checklist

If you can do the following, then you are ready to proceed to the next chapter:

- Understand the concept of classes.
- Know how to call a method
- List and understand at least three types of variables in C#.
- Understand the difference between **private** and **public** variables.
- Answer at least 7 out of 10 of the questions correctly in the quiz.

2
CREATING YOUR FIRST SCRIPT

In this section we will start to code C# scripts in Unity. Some of the objectives of this section will be to:

- Introduce C# scripting in Unity.
- Explain some basic scripting concepts.
- Explain how to display information from the code to the **Console** window.

After completing this chapter, you will be able to:

- Understand basic concepts in C#.
- Understand best coding practices.
- Code your first script in Unity.
- Create classes, methods and variables.
- Instantiate objects based on your own classes.
- Use built-in methods.
- Use conditional statements.

You can skip this chapter if you are already familiar with C#, or if you have already created and used C# scripts within Unity.

QUICK OVERVIEW OF THE INTERFACE

Throughout this book you will be using different windows in Unity; each of these windows includes a label (usually in the top-left corner of the window), and all can be moved around, if necessary, by either changing the layout (**Window | Layouts | ...**) or by dragging and dropping the corresponding tab for a window (this will move the view to where you would like it to appear within the window). In the default layout, the following views appear onscreen (as described in the next screenshot, clockwise from the top left corner):

1. The **Hierarchy** window (the corresponding shortcut is *CTRL+4*): this window (or view) lists all the objects currently present in your scene; these could include, for example, basic shapes, 3D characters, or terrains. This view also makes it possible to identify a hierarchy between objects; for example, we can see in this view if some objects have children or parents (we will explore this concept later).

2. The **Scene** view (*CTRL+1*): this window displays the content of a scene (or the item listed in the **Hierarchy** view) so that you can visualize them and modify them accordingly using the mouse (e.g., move, scale, etc.).

3. The **Game** view (*CTRL+2*): this window makes it possible to visualize the scene as it will appear in the game (i.e., through the lenses of the active camera).

4. The **Inspector** view (*CTRL+3*): this window displays information (i.e., properties) on the object currently selected.

5. The **Console** window (*SHIFT+CTRL+C*): this window displays messages either printed from the code by the user (using keywords) or by Unity. These include warnings or error messages related to your project or code.

6. The **Project** window (*CTRL+5*): this window includes all the assets available and used for your project. These include 3D models, sounds, or textures.

Creating your First Script

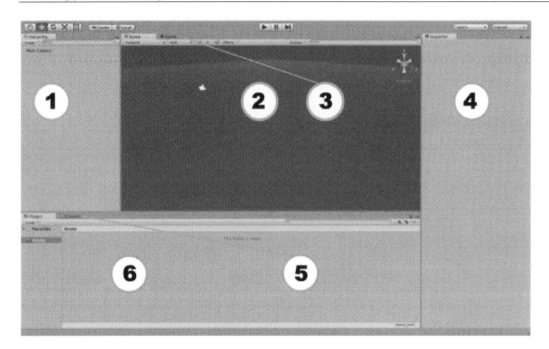

Figure 2-1: Main windows and views in Unity

If you need to know more about how to use common views and shortcuts in Unity, you may download the first book in the series: **Unity from Zero to Proficiency (Foundations).**

Creating your First Script

GETTING STARTED

In Unity, a script (C# script) is usually linked to an object; although it can also be used as a standalone class to be instantiated at a later stage; generally, for your script to be executed, it will need to be linked to an object. So to start with, we will create an empty object, create a script, and link this script to the object.

- Please launch Unity.

- Create a new Project (**File | New Project**).

- Create a new scene (**File | New Scene**).

- Create an empty object (**GameObject | Create Empty**).

- Rename this object: **example_for_scripting** in the **Hierarchy** window. To do so, you can either right-click on this object and then select the option **Rename**, from the contextual menu, or select the object (i.e., click once on it) and press *CTRL + Enter*.

- You will notice, looking at the **Inspector** window, that this object has only one component (**Transform**).

Let's create a new script:

- In the **Project** window, click once on the **Assets** folder.

- Create a new folder to store the scripts (this is not compulsory but it will help to organize your scripts): Select **Create | Folder**.

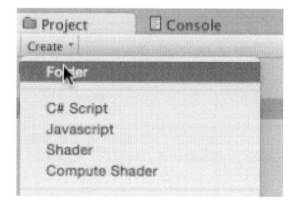

Figure 2-2: Creating a new folder

- This will create a new folder labeled **Folder**.

[77]

Creating your First Script

- Rename this folder **Scripts**.

- Double click on this folder to display its content and so that the script that we are about to create is added to this folder.

- In the **Project** window, select **Create | C# Script**.

- This should create a new **C#** script.

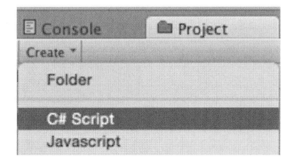

Figure 2-3: Creating a new C# script

- By default, this script will be named **NewBehaviourScript**. However, the name will be highlighted in blue so that you modify the name before the content of the script is created. Please rename this script **MyFirstScript**.

> Note that the name of the script should always match the name of the main class within the script; so if you want to rename this script later on, you will also need to modify the name of the main class within the script.

- Click once on the script; as you do so, look at the **Inspector** window, and you will see the content of the script. By default, you will notice that it includes a definition for the class **MyFirstScript**, namespaces, as well as two different member methods **Start** and **Update**.

- Double-click on the script (within the **Project** window), this will open the script in **MonoDevelop**, which is the default editor for Unity.

> Note that you can change to the editor of your choice (e.g., Notepad++ or Sublime). This can be done by changing Unity's preferences (**Edit | Preferences | External Tool**). This being said, while Mono Develop provides code auto completion by default, this may not be the case for other code editors (e.g., with Sublime, you need to install a specific package).

- As the script is opened in Mono Develop we can see it in more detail. Again, the **Start** method is called at the start of the scene, once. The method **Update** is called every time the screen is refreshed (every frame).

Creating your First Script

- These functions are case-sensitive; because they are built-in functions (i.e., functions made available by Unity for your use), Unity is expecting them to be spelt with the exact spelling and case; otherwise, it will assume that the method that you write serves a different purpose (i.e., we will come back to this type of error later-on).

So let's start coding.

- First let's create a variable of type **integer** called **number** as a private member variable.
- Type the following code just before the method **Start**:

```
private int number;
```

- As you can see, the variable is declared outside any method but inside the class **MyFirstScript**, which means that it is a member variable. The access modifier **private** specifies that the variable is accessible only by the class **MyFirstScript**.
- Then, we can declare a **String** variable called **myName**. Type the following code just after the previous declaration.

```
private string myName;
```

- Then type the following code inside the method **Start** (i.e., anywhere within its curly brackets).

```
number = 1;
```

- This code sets the variable **number** to 1; this variable was declared at the start of the script, as a member variable and it can be accessed from anywhere within the class **MyFirstScript**, including from inside the method **Start**.
- Then type the following code inside the method **Start** after the previous statement (you can replace the word **Patrick** with your own name if you wish):

```
myName = "Patrick";
```

- As you type this line, make sure that the name of the variable is spelt properly with proper case (i.e., upper-case **N**).
- Then type the following code after the previous statement to display a message in the **Console** window.

```
print ("Hello" + myName + "Your number is "+number);
```

- This should print the message **"Hello Patrick Your number is 1"** in the **Console** window in Unity. This window displays error messages from Unity or messages from the code. You may notice the quotes around the word **Patrick**, this means that the text **Hello** will be displayed and we will add the value of the variable **myName** to it. So these two strings will be concatenated (i.e., grouped) to form a dynamic sentence for which the content will depend on the value of the variables **myName** and **number**.

Creating your First Script

So at this stage, your code should look as follows (and if it doesn't, you can use the next code snippet as a template):

```
using UnityEngine;
using System.Collections;
public class MyFirstScript : MonoBehaviour
{
      // Use this for initialization
      private int number;
      private string name;
      void Start ()
      {
          number = 1;
          myName = "Patrick";
          print ("Hello"+ myName + "Your number is "+number);
      }
      // Update is called once per frame
      void Update ()
      {

      }
}
```

- At this stage, we can save our script (*CTRL + S*) and go back to Unity (*ALT + TAB*).

- In Unity, drag and drop the script **MyFirstScript** onto the empty object **example_for_scripting**, as illustrated on the next figure.

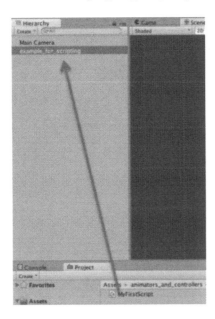

Figure 2-4: Linking the script to an object

[80]

Creating your First Script

- After this, if you click on the object **example_for_scripting** in the hierarchy, you should now see in the **Inspector** window that the script has become a component of this object.

- Look at the **Console** window to see if there are any errors; the window should be empty (i.e., no errors). If there are any warnings, you can leave them for the time being (it won't stop the scene from playing).

- We can now play the scene (*CTRL + P*); as we play the scene and look at the **Console** window (*SHIFT + CTRL + C*), we should see the message "**Hello Patrickyour number is 1**".

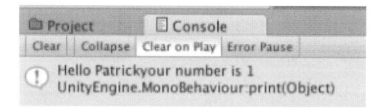

Figure 2-5: Displaying a message in the Console window - part 1

- You may notice a missing space between the words **Patrick** and **you**, and we can correct this accordingly. To do so, we can go back to your code editor (e.g., **Mono Develop**) to modify the script and add spaces as follows (after the words **Hello** and **is,** and before the word **your**):

```
print("Hello " + myName + " your number is "+number);
```

> As we go back to Unity, we can clear the **Console** window by clicking on the tab called **Clear**, as highlighted on the next figure. However, so that the **Console** window is cleared every time we run the scene, we can also click on the tab labeled **Clear on Play**. This ensures that the **Console** window is cleared every time the scene is played, avoiding cluttering the **Console** window with messages that may be obsolete or irrelevant.

- As we play the scene, we can see that the message has been modified to include a space between the words **Patrick** and **your**.

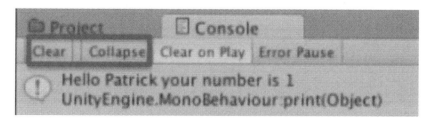

Figure 2-6: Displaying a message in the console window - part 2

[81]

Creating your First Script

This is it! We have created our first script using the built-in method **Start** and some variables, more specifically global variables. These variables are of type **integer** and **String**. Again, these variables are global as they were declared at the start of the script and outside any method. They can, as a result, be used across the script. The full script should look as described on the next code snippet.

```
using UnityEngine;
using System.Collections;
public class MyFirstScript : MonoBehaviour
{
    // Use this for initialization
    private int number;
    private string myName;

    void Start ()
    {
        number = 1;
        myName = "Patrick";
        print("Hello "+ myName + "Your number is " +number);
    }
    // Update is called once per frame
    void Update ()
    {

    }
}
```

USING THE UPDATE FUNCTION

Let's now use the method **Update** to display another message in the **Console** window. Again, this method is called every frame (i.e., every time the screen is refreshed), so any message printed within this method will be displayed indefinitely and every frame.

- Switch to Unity.

- Double click on the script **MyFirstScript** to open it.

- In **Mono Develop** (or any other code editor of your choice), type the following code within the curly brackets of the method **Update**:

```
print (myName);
```

- Save your code (*CTRL + S* or *APPLE + S* for Mac users).

- Switch to Unity and play the scene (*CTRL + P*).

- You should see that the message **Patrick** (or your own name) is displayed indefinitely. In the next figure, we can see that the message is displayed 148 times after a few seconds.

Figure 2-7: Using the "Collapse" option – part 1

- So the code is working well; however, because the message is displayed so many times, we have lost sight of the first message displayed from the **Start** function. This is because the console is flooded by hundreds of identical messages, and we could, to clear up the console, click on the tab labeled **Collapse** within the **Console** window.

> The **Collapse** option ensures that identical messages are displayed only once, along with a number that indicates how many times they have been listed.

- If we stop the game, press the **Collapse** option, and play the scene again, the **Console** window should look as described in the following figure.

Figure 2-8: Using the "Collapse" option - part 2

- As we can see, the message from the **Start** method is displayed (once), whereas the message from the **Update** method is displayed once but the consoles indicates that it has been issued 223 times.

CREATING LOCAL VARIABLES

At this stage, the code is working well, and we have created two member variables: **number** and **myName**. These two variables are accessible throughout our class; however, to experiment with local variables, we could also create variables that are only accessible from one method. So let's experiment.

- Switch back to your code editor (e.g., Mono Develop).

- Delete or comment the code we have just created in the **Start** function. To comment code, you can use double forward slashes, as described in the next code snippet.

Creating your First Script

```
//print (myName);
```

- Add the following code to the method **Start**, just before the closing bracket for this function.

```
int localVariable = 3;
print("local variable: "+localVariable);
```

With the first statement, we declare a variable that should only be used locally, that is to say, within the method **Start**. We then print the value of this variable and display a message that includes the string **"local variable"** that will be followed by (or appended to) the value of the variable **localVariable**; in our case, this should display **"local variable: 3"**.

- Check the code that you have written and ensure that it is correct (e.g., semi-colon at the end of each line).

- Save your script.

- Switch back to Unity and play the scene.

- As we play the scene, the **Console** window should look like the following:

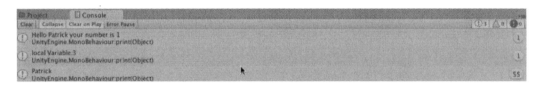

Figure 2-9: Displaying a local variable in the Console window

- We can see the first message from the **Start** method along with the second message that we have just created. Then the message from the **Update** method is displayed (55 times at this stage).

- Now, just to demonstrate the importance of variable scope, we will make an error on purpose; we will try to use the variable **myVariable** (which is a local variable) outside the method **Start**, where it has initially been declared. As you may have guessed, this should trigger an error.

- Switch back to **Mono Develop**.

- Type or copy and paste the following code inside the method **Update**.

```
print("local variable: "+localVariable);
```

- Save your script (*CTRL + S*).

- Switch back to Unity. Before you can try to play the scene, you will notice an error in the **Console** window as follows.

Creating your First Script

Figure 2-10: Generating an error on purpose

By displaying this message, Unity is telling us that it does not recognize the variable **localVariable** in the context where it is being used. This is because it was declared locally in the **Start** method and then used outside this method. So if you see similar messages as you code your game, always check the scope of your variable. This should save you some headaches. :-)

- Switch back to your code editor and comment or delete the line we just created in the **Update** method.

```
//print("local variable "+localVariable);
```

In C# you can comment a line of code by adding // to the start of the line. This means that the code will be part of the script, but it will not be executed.

CREATING A SIMPLE COUNTER

Let's create a simple counter to practice declaring and assigning values to variables. This timer will just count from 0 onwards and use a variable for which the value will be increased overtime (i.e., every frame).

- Switch back to **MonoDevelop** by pressing *ALT + Tab (or CMD + Tab* for Mac users*)*.

As you will have to switch from Unity to **Mono Develop** (or another code editor) a couple of times during development, you can use this shortcut to do so, and it will save you a good bit of time. Imagine saving three seconds 300 times a day! So by pressing *ALT + Tab* (or *APPLE + Tab* on a Mac computer) you can switch back to the previous window (or the application that you were using). By keeping *ALT* pressed and then successively pressing the tab key several times, you can see and select the applications that are currently running on your computer.

- Add the following line at the top of our class (i.e., **MyFirstScript**) to declare our counter (just after the declaration for **myName**).

```
private int counter;
```

- Then, initialize the variable **counter** to **zero** by adding the following code within the **Start** method.

[85]

Creating your First Script

```
counter = 0;
```

> Note that this is done in the **Start** method only for now, so that it is done only once (i.e., at the start of the scene). If we were to add this code to the **Update** method instead, the variable would be initialized to 0 every frame (constantly), and we don't want this right now.

- Finally, add the following code at the end of the **Update** method so that we add one to the current value of the variable **counter** every frame (i.e., every time the screen is refreshed) and display its value.

```
counter = counter + 1;
print ("counter="+counter);
```

- After you have made these modifications, the code should look as follows:

```
using UnityEngine;
using System.Collections;
public class MyFirstScript : MonoBehaviour
{
    // Use this for initialization
    private int number;
    private string myName;
    private int counter;

    void Start ()
    {
        number = 1;
        myName = "Patrick";
        print("Hello "+ myName + "Your number is " +number);

        int localVariable = 3;
        print("local variable: "+localVariable);
        counter = 0;
    }

    // Update is called once per frame
    void Update ()
    {
        counter = counter + 1;
        print ("counter="+counter);
    }
}
```

- Switch back to Unity (*ALT + TAB*).

- Look at the **Console** window: it should not display any error (i.e., provided that you have commented or deleted the code that we created to generate an error on purpose).

- Play the scene (*CTRL + P*), look at the **Console** window, and you should see that the value of the counter is displayed and that it is increasing.

> You may notice that, even if you press the **Collapse** option in the **Console** window, the messages are not collapsed and that they still flood the **Console** window. This is because the **Collapse** option works only when the exact same message is displayed several times; however, in our case, the message differs every frame as the value of the counter is different every time (e.g., "counter=1", "counter=2", etc.).

At this stage we know about local and global variables, so let's look into methods and create our very first method.

CREATING YOUR FIRST METHOD

So what is a method? A method (what we used to call function in JavaScript) is usually employed to perform a task outside the main body of the game. I usually compare functions to a friend or a colleague to whom you gently ask to perform a task for you. In many cases you will call them and they will perform the task. Sometime they will need some particular information to perform the task (e.g., a number to be able to call someone on your behalf); some other times, they will call you back to give you the information that they found, but in other cases, this may not be necessary, and they will perform the task without contacting you afterwards.

So there are essentially three types of methods:

- Methods that just perform actions with no parameters.

- Methods that perform actions with parameters.

- Methods that perform actions (with or without a parameter) and return a result.

DECLARING A METHOD

If you have coded in JavaScript before, functions were declared using the keyword **function**; however, in C# a method declaration usually requires an access modifier, the type of data returned, and the type of the parameters passed to this function.

The syntax to declare a method is as follows:

- The access modifier (e.g., private, public, or protected).

- The type of data returned by the method (e.g., **float**, **string** or **bool**).

- The name of the method.

- Opening round brackets.

- The type of the parameters and their name.

- Closing round brackets.

- Any action (i.e., statement) performed by this method will be added within the curly brackets and followed by a semi-colon.

In the next sections, we will see examples of how methods can be declared.

METHODS THAT DON'T RETURN OR TAKE ANY PARAMETER

In this case, the method is called with no parameter; it will then perform an action. This is the simplest form of methods. The syntax is as follows: the access modifier, the keyword **void**, followed by the **name of the function**, followed by **opening and closing round brackets**, followed by **opening and closing curly brackets**. Any action (i.e., statement) performed by this function will be added within the curly brackets and followed by a semi-colon.

```
public void theNameOfyourMethod()
{
}
```

The keyword **void** indicates that the method does not return any data.

So to create our first method, we could type the following at the end of our script (i.e., before the last closing curly brackets):

```
public void myFirstMethod()
{
    print ("Hello World");
}
```

When called, this method will print the message **"Hello World"** to the **Console** window.

At this stage we have just defined the method **myFirstMethod**; in other words, we have specified what the method should do when it has been called. So once the method has been defined, we can call it using the syntax: **nameOfTheMethod();** for example, to call **myFirstMethod** from any other method within the script, we could write the following statement at the end of the **Start** method:

```
myFirstMethod();
```

So that this message stands out in the **Console** window, we can comment all other **print** statements inside the **Start** method so that the code of your script looks like this (the changes are highlighted in bold):

```csharp
using UnityEngine;
using System.Collections;
public class MyFirstScript : MonoBehaviour
{
    // Use this for initialization
    private int number;
    private string myName;
    private int counter;

    void Start ()
    {
        number = 1;
        myName = "Patrick";
        //print("Hello "+ myName + "Your number is " +number);

        int localVariable = 3;
        //print("local variable: "+localVariable);
        counter = 0;
        myFirstMethod();
    }

    // Update is called once per frame
    void Update ()
    {
        counter = counter + 1;
        //print ("counter="+counter);

    }
    public void myFirstMethod()
    {
        print ("Hello World");
    }
}
```

Creating your First Script

> You may wonder why the methods **Update** and **Start** do not include any access modifier (e.g., public or private). This is because by default, the access modifier for a member method in C# is private. So if no access modifier is specified for a method, it will be treated as a private method.
>
> Note that the location of the method in the script (i.e., at the end or at the start) does not matter, as long as it is declared within the class (**MyFirstScript**) and outside any another method: so you need to declare your method outside of any other methods (i.e., after the closing curly bracket for a method or before the method); we could have easily written this method at the start or middle of the script, resulting in no errors.

- Check that your code is written properly (i.e., error-free).
- Save your code (*CTRL + S*).
- Switch to Unity (*ALT + TAB*).
- Check that there are no errors in the **Console** window.
- Play the scene and check that the message says **"Hello World"**.

DEFINING A METHOD THAT TAKES PARAMETERS

So far, we looked at methods that would not take or return any parameters. For now, we will create a method that still doesn't return any data, but that takes one or several parameters in order to perform calculations.

So to borrow the previous example, you call someone, give them some information, and ask them to perform an action based on your instructions. To illustrate this concept, let's create a new method that will display a message based on a parameter passed as an argument.

- Please type the following code at the end of the class (i.e., before the last closing curly bracket).

```
public void mySecondMethod(string name)
{
    print ("Hello, your name is " +name);
}
```

- In the previous code, we have created a method called **mySecondMethod**. It takes a parameter called **name** of type **String** (i.e., text). So when we call this method and include a string variable within the brackets, this variable will be referred as **name** within this method.
- Let me illustrate with the following code.

Creating your First Script

```
mySecondMethod("Patrick");
```

If we were to type the previous code inside the **Start** method, the method **mySecondMethod** would set the variable **name** with the string **Patrick**, and then display the message **Hello Patrick**. The variable **name** is a local variable to the method **mySecondFunction**.

If you have not already done so, please add the following code to the **Start** method. You can replace the word **Patrick** with your own name.

```
mySecondMethod("Patrick");
```

- Save your code, switch to Unity, check the **Console** window for any error and play the scene.

- You should see, amongst other messages, the message **"Hello, your name is Patrick"**.

- You could now change the call to this method and pass your own name as a parameter and see the result as you play the scene.

Note that we could have created a method that takes many other parameters. For example, we could have created a method that takes the first and last names as parameters, as follows.

```
public void myThirdMethod(string fName, string lName)
{
        print ("Hello, your name is " +fName+" "+lName);
}
```

DEFINING A METHOD THAT TAKES PARAMETERS AND RETURNS INFORMATION

So far we know how to declare a method that takes parameters; however we have not yet seen how we could define a method that also returns information.

This type of method, will, in addition to possibly taking parameters and processing this information, return information back to where it was called.

In the following example, we will create a method that does all three: it will be called; it will then take the **year of birth** as a parameter, and then calculate and return the corresponding **age** (based on the current year).

- Please add the following code at the end of the script.

```
public int calculateAge(int YOB)
{
    int age;
    age = 2016 - YOB;
    return (age);
}
```

In the previous code:

- The method called **calculateAge** is declared using the keywords **public** and **int** as its access type is **public** and as it will return an **integer**.

- The method called **calculateAge** takes a parameter called **YOB** (short for Year Of Birth).

- The method **calculateAge** then subtracts **YOB** from the current year and returns the result.

Please add the following code to the method **Start**.

```
int myAge = calculateAge(1998);
print("Your age is " + myAge);
```

In the previous code:

- The method **calculateAge** is called once; it returns the calculated age, and this (returned) value is saved in the variable called **myAge**.

- This variable **myAge** is then printed in the **Console** window.

- Save your code, and switch back to Unity.

- Check that there are no errors in the **Console** window and play the scene.

- The console should display, amongst other messages, the message **"Your age is 18"**.

As you can see, there are different types of methods that you can create, depending on your needs. They may or may not take parameters, and they may or may not return values.

CREATING YOUR OWN CLASS

To complete this section, it would be great to see how you could create and use your own class. So, we will simply create a class for a bike and also use it. So, let's get started.

- Please create a new C# script called **Bike** (i.e., select **Create | C# Script** from the **Project** window).

- This should generate a script with the following code by default:

```csharp
using UnityEngine;
using System.Collections;

public class Bike : MonoBehaviour {

    // Use this for initialization
    void Start () {

    }

    // Update is called once per frame
    void Update () {

    }
}
```

When this is done, let's edit this script to add some features to our bike.

- We can start by deleting the text **:MonoBehaviour**. This is because our class will be used as a standalone and not inherit from the **MonoBehaviour** class (which is mainly for game objects in the scene).

- Then we can delete the methods Start and Update, for the same reason as explained above, as we will create our own methods for our class Bike.

- So your code should look like the following:

Creating your First Script

```
using UnityEngine;
using System.Collections;

public class Bike
{


}
```

At this stage we have a blank canvas that we can use for our new class.

- Please add the following code at the start of the class (just before the comment "**Use this for initialization**"). The new code is highlighted in bold.

```
using UnityEngine;
using System.Collections;

public class Bike
{
    private string name;
    private float speed;
    private int nbWheels;
}
```

- In the previous code, we declare three private member variables of type **string**, **float** and **int**. These will be used to identify the name, speed and number of wheels for the bike created.

We now need to define one or more constructors for our class, to define the feature of each new bike created. Please add the following code within the class:

```
//First Constructor
public Bike()
{
        name = "Just another bike";
        speed = 0.0f;
}
//Second Constructor
public Bike(string newName)
{
        name = newName;
        speed = 0.0f;
        Debug.Log ("Just created a new bike with the name" + name);

}
```

- In the previous code, we create two constructors; both methods are public and their names are the same as the name of our class (i.e., Bike).

> The method **print** that we used earlier is only accessible for classes that inherit from the class **MonoBehaviour**; in our case, we have removed this inheritance (our class does not inherit anymore from the class **MonoBehaviour**), so we use the method **Debug.Log** instead which is accessible from the library **UnityEngine** that we imported at the start of our script); this is equivalent to the method **print**.

- The first constructor will be used if the object is created but no parameters are used at its instantiation. We see that, by default, we just set the name of this bike to "**Just another bike**" and its speed to **0**. This constructor will be called if we use the following code to create a new bike.

```
Bike bike1 = new Bike();
```

- The next constructor takes a **string** as a parameter; which means that it will be called if we create a new bike and pass a string as a parameter when an object is created from this class (i.e., instantiated). We see that if this is the case, the name of the bike will be set to (or initialized with) the parameter passed to this constructor and its speed will be set to **0**. This constructor will be called if we use the following code to create a new bike.

```
Bike bike2 = new Bike("Name of the Bike");
```

So your code should look like the following by now (if not, you can use the next code as a template).

```
using UnityEngine;
using System.Collections;

public class Bike
{
    private string name;
    private float speed;
    private int nbWheels;

    //First Constructor
    public Bike()
    {
        name = "Just another bike";
        speed = 0.0f;
    }
    //Second Constructor
    public Bike(string newName)
    {
        name = newName;
        speed = 0.0f;
        Debug.Log ("Just created a new bike with the name " + name);
    }
}
```

So, once you have created our new class, we could now test it by doing the following:

- Open the script **MyFirstScript**.

- Add the following code in the **Start** method.

```
Bike b1 = new Bike ("My First Bike");
```

- Save your script.

- Play the scene.

- You should see that the **Console** window displays the message **"Just created a new bike with the name My First Bike"**.

So at this stage, while we have created constructors, we could also create methods that make it possible to modify some of the attributes of our bike.

For example, we could add the following method to the class **Bike**.

Creating your First Script

```
public void accelerate ()
{
    speed+=1;
    Debug.Log ("Our new speed is now" + speed);
}
```

We can then modify the **Start** method in the script MyFirstScript as follows (new code in bold).

```
Bike b1 = new Bike ("My First Bike");
```
b1.accelerate();
b1.accelerate();

Save this code, and play the scene. You should see two additional messages in the **Console** window saying **"Our new speed is now 1"** and **"Our new speed is now 2"**.

COMMON ERRORS AND THEIR MEANING

As you will start your journey through C# coding, you may sometimes find it difficult to interpret the errors produced by Unity in the console. However, after some practice, you will manage to recognize them, to understand (and also avoid) them, and to fix them accordingly. The next list identifies the errors that my students often come across when they start coding in C#.

When an error occurs, Unity usually provides you with enough information to check where it has occurred, so that you can fix it. While many are relatively obvious to spot, some others are trickier to find. In the following, I have listed some of the most common errors that you will come across as you start with C#. The trick is to recognize the error message so that you can understand what Unity is trying to tell you. Again, this is part of the learning process, and you **WILL** make these mistakes, but as you see these errors, you will learn to understand them (and avoid them too :-)). Again, Unity is trying to help you by communicating, to the best that it can, where the issue is; by understanding the error messages we can get to fix these bugs easily. So that it is easier to fix errors, Unity usually provides the following information when an error occurs:

- Name of the script where the error was found.

- The number of the row and column where the error was found.

- A description of the error that was found.

So, if Unity was to generate the following message "**Assets/Scripts/MyFirstScript.cs (23,34) BCE0085: Unknown identifier: 'localVariable'**", it is telling us that an error has occurred in the script called **MyFirstScript**, at the line **23**, and around the **34th** character (i.e., column) on this line. In this particular message, it is telling us that it can't recognize the variable **localVariable**.

So, you may come across the following errors (this list is also available in the resource pack as a pdf file, so that you can print it and keep it close by):

- "**;**" **expected**: This error could mean that you have forgotten to add a semi-colon at the end of a statement. To fix this error, just go to the line mentioned in the error message and ensure that you add a semi-colon.

- **Unknown identifier**: This error could mean that Unity does not know the variable that you are mentioning. It can be due to at least three reasons: (1) the variable has not been declared yet, (2) the variable has been declared but outside the scope of the method (e.g., declared locally in a different function), or (3) the name of the variable that you are using is incorrect (i.e., spelling or case). Remember, the names of all variables and functions are case-sensitive; so by just using an incorrect case, Unity will assume that you refer to another variable, which, in this case, has not been declared yet.

- **The best method overload for function ... is not compatible**: This error is probably due to the fact that you are trying to call a function and to pass a parameter with a type that is not what Unity is expecting. For example, the method **mySecondMethod**, described in the next code snippet, is expecting a **String** value for its parameter; so, if you pass an integer value instead, an error will be generated.

```
void mySecondFunction(string name)
{
        print ("Hello, your name is" +name);
}
mySecondFunction("John");//this is correct
mySecondFunction(10);//this will trigger an error
```

- **Expecting } found ...:** This error is due to the fact that you may have forgotten to either close or open curly brackets. This can be the case for conditional statements or functions. To avoid this issue, there is a trick (or best practice) that you can use: you can ensure that you indent your code so that corresponding opening and closing brackets are at the same level. In the next example, you can see that the brackets corresponding to the start and end of the method **testBrackets** are indented at the same level, and so are the brackets for each of the conditional statements within this function. By indenting your code (using several spaces or tabulation), you can make sure that your code is clear and that missing curly brackets are easier to spot.

```
void testBrackets()
{
        if (myVar == 2)
        {
                print ("Hello World");
                myVar = 4;
        }
        else
        {
        }
}
```

Sometimes, although the syntax of your code is correct and does not yield any error in the **Console** window, it looks like nothing is happening; in other words, it looks like the code, and especially the methods that you have created do not work. This is bound to happen as you create your first scripts. It can be quite frustrating (and I have been there :-)) because, in this case, Unity will not let us know where the error is. However, there is a succession of checks that you can perform to ensure that this does not happen; so you could check the following:

- The script that you have written has been saved.

- The script has no errors.

- The script is attached to an object.

- If the script is indeed attached to an object and you are using a built-in method that depends on the type of object it is attached to, make sure that the script is linked to the correct object. For example, if your script is using the built-in method

OnControllerColliderHit, which is used to detect collision between the **FPSController** and other objects, but you don't drag and drop the script on the **FPSController** object, the script, while being error-free, will not be used, and the method **OnControllerColliderHit** will not be called if you collide with an object.

- If the script is indeed attached to the right object and is using a built-in method such as **Start**, or **Update**, make sure that these functions are spelt properly (i.e., exact spelling and case). For example for the method **Update**, what happens here is that the system will call the method **Update** every frame, and no other function. So if you write a method spelt **update**, the system will look for the **Update** function, and since it has not been defined (or overwritten), nothing will happen, unless you specifically call this function. The same would happen for the method **Start**. In both cases, the system will assume that you have created two new functions **update** and **start**.

BEST PRACTICES

To ensure that your code is easy to understand and that it does not generate countless headaches when trying to modify it, there are a few good practices that you can start applying as your begin with coding; these should save you some time along the line.

Variable naming

- Use meaningful names that you can understand, especially after leaving your code for two weeks.

```
string myName = "Patrick";//GOOD
string b = "Patrick";//NOT SO GOOD
```

- Capitalize words within a name consistently (e.g., camel or Pascal casing).

```
bool testIfTheNameIsCorrect;// GOOD
bool testifthenameiscorrect; // NOT SO GOOD
```

Methods

- Check that all opening brackets have a corresponding closing bracket.
- Indent your code.
- Comment your code as much as possible to explain how it works.
- Use the **Start** method if something just needs to be done once at the start of the game.
- If something needs to be done repeatedly, then the method **Update** might be a better option.

LEVEL ROUNDUP

Summary

In this chapter, we have become familiar with different programming concepts. We also looked into classes, constructors, and member variables. Finally, we created our first script class and experimented instantiating instances and displaying their properties. In the next chapter, we will harness these skills to bring interactivity to our own 3D environment.

Quiz

It is now time to test your knowledge. Please answer the following questions. The answers are available on the next page.

1. A class can have more than two constructors.
2. Different constructors can have the same name.
3. A public variable can be accessed from anywhere in your programme.
4. When a new instance of an object is created, the corresponding constructor is called.
5. All classes created with Unity will inherit from the **Monobehaviour** class by default.
6. The name of a C# script, when created, will be the same for the class defined within this file.
7. So that it can be called from anywhere outside the class, a **getter** needs to be declared as public.
8. In C# the default access type for member variables and methods is **internal**.
9. In **camel casing** the first character of each word is capitalized except for the first word.
10. In **Pascal casing** the first character of each word is capitalized.

Solutions to the Quiz

1. TRUE.
2. TRUE.
3. TRUE.
4. TRUE.
5. TRUE.
6. TRUE.
7. TRUE.
8. FALSE.
9. TRUE.
10. TRUE.

Checklist

If you can do the following, then you are ready to go to the next chapter:

- Create a new C# script.
- Attach a script to an object.
- Create a class.
- Create member variables.
- Create member methods.
- Call a constructor.
- Know three of the most common coding mistakes, and how to avoid them.
- Know how to comment your code in a script.
- Answer at least 7 out of 10 of the questions correctly in the quiz.

Challenge 1

Now that you have managed to complete this chapter and that you have improved your skills, let's put these to the test.

- Modify your code to create two additional member methods.
- Instantiate objects and call these methods from these objects.

Challenge 2

In this challenge, you will create your own constructor.

- Modify your code to create one additional constructor.
- Instantiate objects based on this constructor.

3
ADDING SIMPLE AI

In this section we will discover how you can create very simple Artificial Intelligence (AI) to implement a canon that points in the direction of your character and fires projectiles.

After completing this chapter, you will be able to:

- Instantiate objects.
- Instantiate explosions.
- Make it possible for a canon to follow a particular object.
- Modify the firing rate of the canon.
- Detect collision between the cannon balls and the player and instantiate an explosion on impact.

Adding Simple AI

RESOURCES NECESSARY FOR THIS CHAPTER

To get started with this chapter, you will be using resources that you have downloaded from the companion website. If you have not done so yet, please do the following:

- Open the following link: **http://learntocreategames.com/books/**

- Select this book ("**Unity from Zero to Proficiency - Intermediate**").

- On the new page, click on the link labelled "**Book Files**", or scroll down to the bottom of the page.

- In the section called "**Download your Free Resource Pack**", enter your email address and your first name, and click on the button labeled "**Yes, I want to receive my bonus pack**".

- After a few seconds, you should receive a link to your free start-up pack.

- When you receive the link, you can download all the resources to your computer.

INSTANTIATING PROJECTILES

At this stage, we are getting familiar with Unity and creating C# scripts; we will now get to create a very simple AI object that will target our user and shoot cannon balls in its direction. The workflow will be as follows; we will:

- Create a simple environment.
- Add a third-person controller.
- Add a canon.
- Instantiate cannon balls frequently.
- Ensure that the canon is always facing the target and shoot in its direction.
- Detect when the cannon balls have hit the player and instantiate an explosion at the location of the impact.
- Modify the firing rate of the canon.

So, let's get started:

- Switch back to Unity.
- Select **File | New Project**.

Once the project is open we will add a ground and a Third-Person Controller as follows:

- Create a new box (**GameObject | 3D Object | Cube**).
- Using the **Move** tool or the **Inspector** window, change the position of this object to **(0,0,0)**.
- Using the **Scale** tool or the **Inspector** window, change the **scale** of this object to **(100,1,100)**, this will rescale it on the **x-**, and **z–axes**.
- Rename this box **ground**.

We will then add a **Third-Person Controller**:

- Import the **Characters** assets by selecting **Asset | Import Package | Characters**.

Adding Simple AI

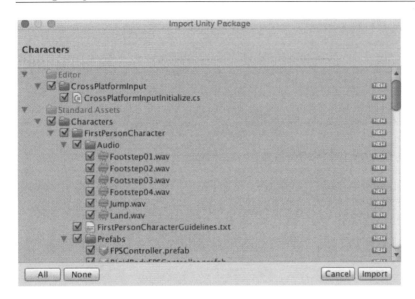

Figure 3-1: Importing the Characters Asset package

- Click **Import** to import all assets in the package.

- Once the import is complete, this will have created a folder called **Characters** in the folder **Assets | Standard Assets**.

- In the **Project** window, navigate to the folder **Assets | Standard Assets | Characters | ThirdPersonCharacter | Prefabs**.

- From this folder, drag and drop the prefab called **ThirdPersonController** to the scene, jus above the box we have created.

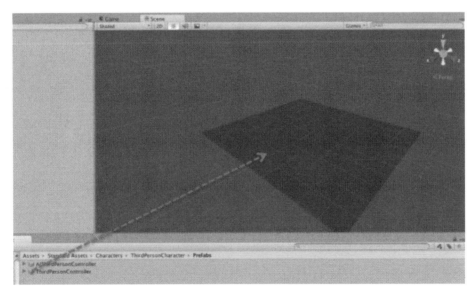

Figure 3-2: Adding a third-person controller

This will add an object called **ThirdPersonController** in the **Hierarchy** window.

And last but not least, we will add a camera that will follow the player:

- Import the **Cameras** assets by selecting **Asset | Import Package | Cameras**.

- Leave all default options (i.e., import all assets in the package) and click **Import**.

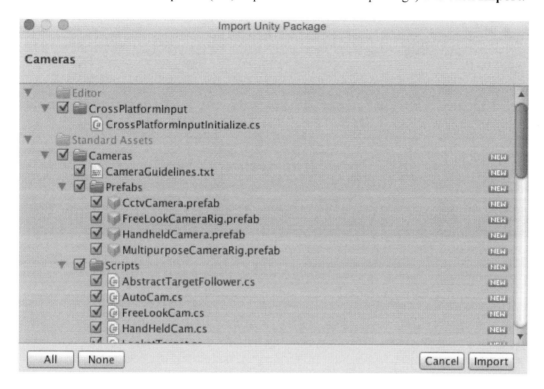

Figure 3-3: Importing the Camera asset package

- Once the import is complete, this will have created a folder called **Cameras** in the folder **Assets | Standard Assets**.

- In the **Project** window, navigate to the folder **Assets | Standard Assets | Cameras | Prefabs**.

- From this folder, drag and drop the prefab called **MultipurposeCameraRig** to the scene.

Adding Simple AI

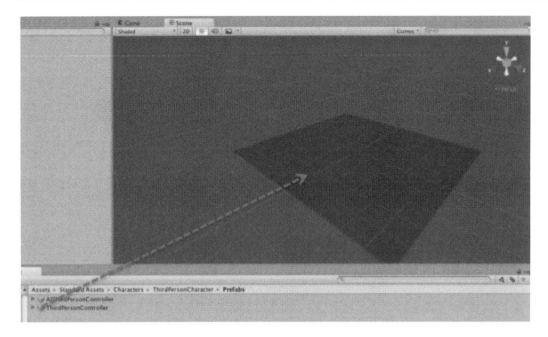

Figure 3-4: Adding a new camera

- This will add an object called **MultipurposeCameraRig** in the **Hierarchy** window.
- Select this object.
- Then drag and drop the object **ThirdPersonController** from the **Hierarchy** window to the field called **target** as described on the next figures.

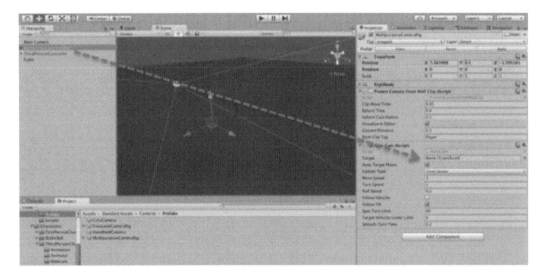

Figure 3-5: Setting-up the camera (part 1)

Adding Simple AI

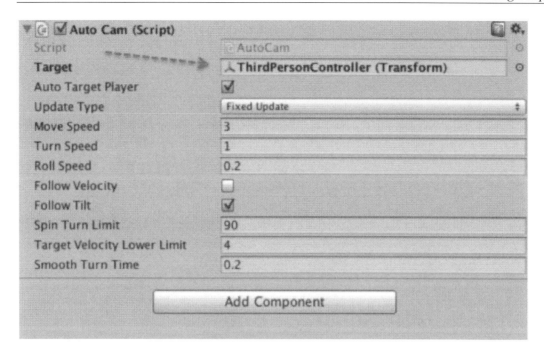

Figure 3-6: Setting-up the camera (part 2)

Finally, we will deactivate the main camera that was present in the scene at the start, since we already have a camera that follows the player, and we will also add some light.

- Select the object called **Main Camera** in the **Hierarchy** window, and, using the **Inspector** window, deactivate this object by unchecking the box located to the left of the name of the object (top-left corner)

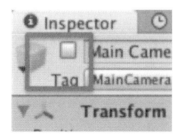

Figure 3-7: Deactivating the main camera

- Select: **Game Object | Light | Directional Light**. This will create a new directional light.
- Change the position of this light to **(0,10,0)** and its rotation to **(0,0,0)**.

So at this stage you should see that the following in the **Hierarchy** window:

- A third-person controller.

[113]

Adding Simple AI

- A **Camera** object that is set to follow this character.
- A **ground** object on which the character will be able to walk or run.
- A light for the scene.

So first, let's play the scene and experiment with the character. As you play the scene, and use the arrow keys on your keyboard, you will be able to move the character in different directions and see that the camera is following this character.

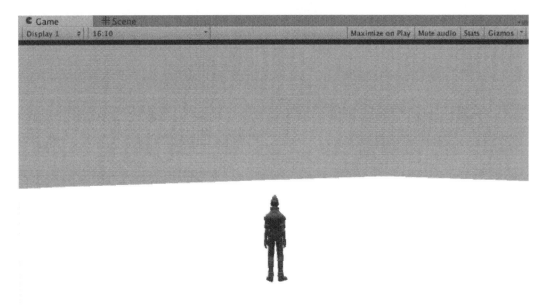

Figure 3-8: Playing the initial scene

You can now stop the scene; we will now create a launcher that will be used to fire projectiles at the character.

- Please create a new cube.
- Rename this cube **launcher**.
- Move it away from the player and make sure that it is at least 1 meter above the ground, for example at the position **(15, 2, 0)**.
- Deactivate the collider component from this object: select the **launcher** and deactivate its collider component in the **Inspector** window. This is so that any object launched through the **launcher** does not collide with it.

Adding Simple AI

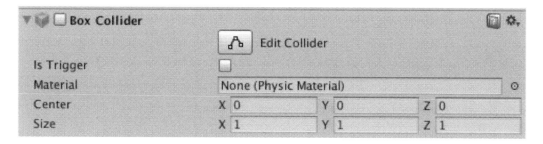

Figure 3-9: Deactivating the collider for the launcher

Next, we will create the actual projectile that will consist of a simple sphere. This sphere will be used as a template for any projectile fired from the launcher.

- Create a new sphere (**Game Object | 3D Object | Sphere**).

- Rename it **ball**.

- Change its scale settings to **(0.2, 0.2, 0.2)** so that its radius is **.2**.

Because this ball will be used as an airborne projectile, it will need to behave as if it was subject to gravity and emulate other physics-based behaviors. For this, we can add what is called a **rigid body** to this object; this is a component that effectively gives physics properties to an object:

- Select the object labeled **ball**.

- From the main menu, select: **Component | Physics | Rigidbody**.

- You should now see in the **Inspector** that a component called **Rigidbody** has been added to the object called **ball**, as described on the next figures.

[115]

Adding Simple AI

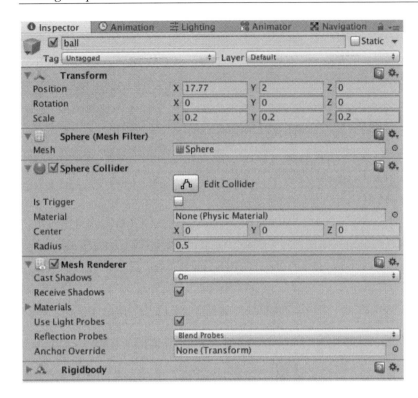

Figure 3-10: Adding a Rigidbody component

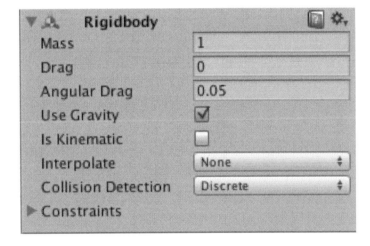

Figure 3-11: Checking the ball's physics properties

From the previous figure, we can see that this object will have a mass of 1 kilogram and that it will be subject to gravity.

Once this is done (i.e., once you have added the **Rigidbody** component), we can now create a prefab with this particular object.

Adding Simple AI

> The idea of a prefab is that sometimes you would like to instantiate or create objects based on a template. So, a prefab can be used as a template and then instantiated when needed.

In our case, we want to create several projectiles, so we will create a prefab that can be used for every projectile.

- In the **Project** window, select the folder called **Assets**.
- Then select the option **Create | Folder** as described on the next figure.

Figure 3-12: Creating a new folder

- This will create a new folder. Rename this folder **launcher** and double-click on it, so that the next asset (i.e., the new prefab) that we create is saved in this folder.
- In the **Project** window, select **Create | Prefab**, this will create a prefab symbolized by a grey cube in the **Project** window (or the folder that was selected before your created your prefab).
- Rename this prefab **projectile**.

Figure 3-13: Adding a prefab

- Drag and drop the object called **ball** (from the **Hierarchy** window) on this prefab; you may notice that the prefab has turned to blue; which means that it now contains an object that can be instantiated (as illustrated on the next figure).

Adding Simple AI

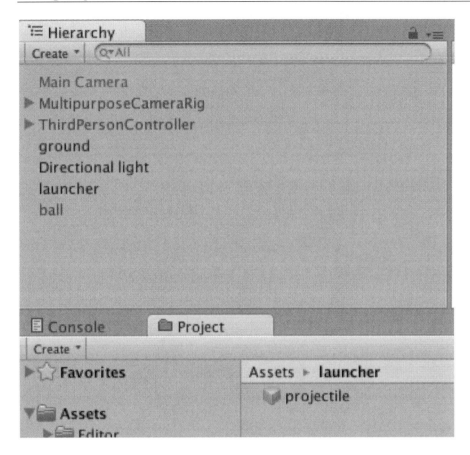

Figure 3-14: Creating a new prefab

Once the prefab has been created, it is time to create a script that will control the launcher and instantiate projectiles.

- From the **Project** window, create a new C# script (**Create | C# Script**) named **LaunchProjectile**.

- Once it has been created, please open this script in your code editor.

The first thing we will do in this script, is to create a member variable that will act as a placeholder for the projectile. So we will create a **public** variable for the projectile's prefab, so that, when the script has been attached to an object, we can drag and drop the prefab to this empty field.

- Please add the following code to the script, within the class definition (new code in bold).

```
using UnityEngine;
using System.Collections;

public class LaunchProjectile : MonoBehaviour
{
    public GameObject projectile;
    // Use this for initialization
    void Start () {

    }

    // Update is called once per frame
    void Update () {

    }
}
```

Then, we can try to detect when the player has pressed a key on the keyboard so that an object (i.e., a projectile) can be instantiated in this case. Please enter the following code within the **Update** function.

```
void Update ()
{
    if (Input.GetKeyDown (KeyCode.P))
    {
        GameObject t = (GameObject) Instantiate (projectile, transform.position, Quaternion.identity);
    }
}
```

In the previous code:

- We check whether the key **P** has been pressed.

- We then create a new **GameObject** using the keyword **Instantiate**. This **GameObject** is created (or instantiated) from the **projectile** prefab; its position will be the same as the object linked to this script (i.e., in our case, this will be the launcher, using **transform.position**), and no rotation will be applied to this new object.

- We also add the keyword **GameObject** before the keyword **Instantiate**; this is to ensure that the object created is of type **GameObject**. In programming terms, it is called **casting**.

Adding Simple AI

> **About casting**: as you will be coding in C#, the compiler will require that every time you create or initialize a variable, that the type of the left side of the **equal** sign is the same as the type on the right side of the equal sign. Using casting can help to ensure that this condition is fulfilled. If you omit to perform this casting, Unity may throw an error that may look like "**Cannot implicitly convert type**". So if you ever get this error message, you may check the types of the variables on either sides of an equal sign and use casting, if need be.

- We can now save our script.
- After checking that it includes no errors, we can then drag and drop it on the object called **launcher** in the **Hierarchy** window.

There is now one last thing we need to do; that is, dragging and dropping the prefab we have created initially on to the field called **projectile** in the script that is attached to the launcher.

- Please select the object **launcher** in the **Hierarchy** window.
- In the **Inspector** window, you should see that there is an empty field, in the component **LaunchProjectile**, called **projectile**.

Figure 3-15: Checking the script LaunchProjectile

- Please drag and drop the **projectile** prefab from the **Project** window to this field; this will effectively set the value of the variable **projectile** in the script to the prefab, as described on the next figure.

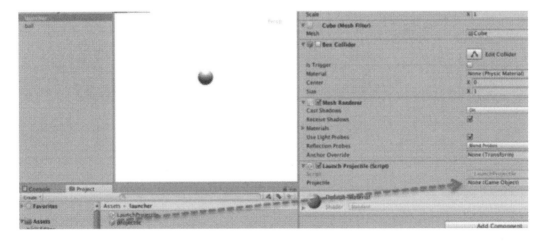

Figure 3-16: Setting a public variable with a prefab

[120]

Adding Simple AI

> Note that we can access this variable because it was previously set as **public** in our script.

Once this is done, let's play the scene and test our script.

- Please play the scene.
- Move the character near the launcher.
- Press the **P** key, and you should notice that balls are dropped from the launcher, as described on the next figure.

Figure 3-17: Testing the launcher

So at this stage, the instantiation is working properly; however, we would like now to add a force to these spheres, so that they are effectively propelled in the air (rather than being dropped on the ground). Before that, there is also another aspect that we need to look at: as we create these projectiles, they may start to overcrowd the scene and we could decide to destroy them after a few seconds, to keep performances high. For this purpose, we will use the method **Destroy**.

- Please add the following code, within the code that tests for the user input (just after the instantiation; the new code is highlighted in bold).

[121]

Adding Simple AI

```
void Update ()
{
    if (Input.GetKeyDown (KeyCode.P))
    {
        GameObject t = (GameObject) Instantiate (projectile, transform.position, Quaternion.identity);
        Destroy (t,3);
    }
}
```

In the previous code, we destroy the ball that has been instantiated after three seconds.

- Please save your code.
- Play the scene.
- Move the character near the launcher.
- Press the **P** key several times.
- Check that the balls that have been created disappear after a few seconds.

We can now start to think about adding a force to the projectiles. To do so, we will be using a method that exists for all rigid bodies, called **AddForce**. This method will add a force to a specific rigid body, based on a direction and a magnitude (i.e., intensity).

- Please add the following code just after the **Destroy** statement that we have added earlier.

```
t.GetComponent<Rigidbody>().AddForce(transform.forward * 500);
```

In the previous code:

- We access the **Rigidbody** component of our object.
- We then add a force forward with an intensity of **500**.

Now, the last modification we will make will be to ensure that the launcher is always facing the player, so that the projectile is launched towards the player. Thankfully, Unity provides a method that makes it possible to look at (or rotate to face) a particular object; this method usually needs a target to look at; in our case this will be the player. So let's create this feature.

- Please add the following code at the beginning of the class.

```
public GameObject target;
```

- This variable will be used as a placeholder so that the player becomes the target for this launcher.
- Then, we can add the following line within the code that tests for the user input.

```
transform.LookAt(target.transform);
```

In this code, we specify that we would like our launcher to look in the direction of the target. This code should be executed before we start to instantiate the projectile, so it needs to be added just at the start of the conditional statement; so the full code should look as follows:

```
using UnityEngine;
using System.Collections;

public class LaunchProjectile : MonoBehaviour
{
    public GameObject projectile;
    public GameObject target;
    // Use this for initialization
    void Start () {

    }

    // Update is called once per frame
    void Update ()
    {
        if (Input.GetKeyDown (KeyCode.P))
        {
            transform.LookAt(target.transform);
            GameObject t = (GameObject) Instantiate (projectile, transform.position, Quaternion.identity);
            t.GetComponent<Rigidbody>().AddForce(transform.forward * 500);
            Destroy (t,3);
        }

    }
}
```

As you save your script, please switch back to Unity and check that the placeholder **target** appears in the **Inspector** window.

We can now set its value:

- Select the launcher in the **Hierarchy** window.

- Drag and drop the object **ThirdPersonController** from the **Hierarchy** window to the variable **target**, in the script attached to the launcher, as described on the next figure.

Adding Simple AI

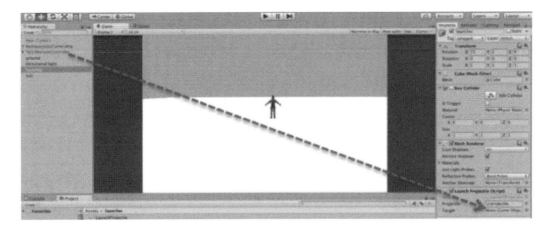

Figure 3-18: Setting the target for the launcher

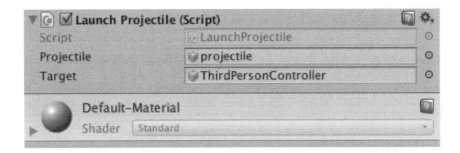

Figure 3-19: Setting the target for the launcher (close-up)

Once this is done we can test the scene, and as you play it, you will see that when you move the character around and press the *P* key, the projectiles will be fired in the direction of the player.

As you do so you may also notice that more force may need to be applied to the projectile if the player is at a medium distance from the launcher. So we could do the following:

- Open the script.

- Modify the following line so that the force applied is 1000 (instead of 500).

```
t.GetComponent<Rigidbody>().AddForce(transform.forward * 1000);
```

Now that we have managed to test whether the launcher could fire projectiles, we can now make it possible for this launcher to automatically fire projectiles (without the need to press a key). For this purpose, we just need to remove the condition (i.e., key pressed). So we can modify the code and remove this conditional statement by either deleting it or commenting it as follows.

```
//if (Input.GetKeyDown (KeyCode.P))
```

After you save your code and as you play the scene, you will notice that the firing range of the launcher has increased significantly.

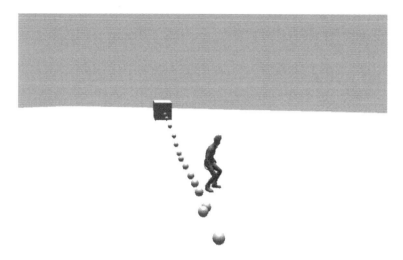

Figure 3-20: Avoiding the projectiles

This being said, there is one aspect of the launcher that we could change; that is, its reload time. At present, the launcher fires projectiles indefinitely, making it relatively difficult for the player not to get hit. What we could do is to add more time between each shot. This time could be set in stone or, to increase challenge, this time could decrease over time (i.e., increasing firing rate). To implement this feature, let's modify the code with the **Update** method as follows:

- First, we can add a member variable **time** that will be used as a timer; please add this code to the start of the class.

```
float time;
```

- Then we can modify the **Update** method as follows (new code highlighted in bold).

Adding Simple AI

```
void Update ()
{
        time +=Time.deltaTime;
        if (time >=2.0)
        {
            time = 0;
            transform.LookAt(target.transform);
            GameObject   t   =   (GameObject)   Instantiate   (projectile,
transform.position, Quaternion.identity);
            t.GetComponent<Rigidbody>().AddForce(transform.forward * 1000);
            Destroy (t,3);
        }
}
```

In the previous code:

- The value of the variable **time** is increased by one every second.
- When it reaches the value **two** it is then initialized back to 0 and a projectile is instantiated.
- As a result, a projectile will be instantiated every two seconds.
- Please save your code, and switch back to Unity.
- Check that there are no errors.
- Play the scene and see how the shooting frequency is now every two seconds.

MANAGING COLLISION

So at this stage, we have managed to implement a relatively simple, yet effective, AI that follows the player and shoots projectiles in his/her direction. We could now modify the code that we have to date to implement the following:

- Collision detection for the projectile.

- An explosion is created at the point of impact.

- If the collision is with the player, then the player is destroyed.

So let's get started:

- Please create a new C# script and name it **CollisionWithProjectile**. You can create this new file in the folder called **launcher** or any other folder of your choice.

- Please open the script and add the following code at the beginning of the class.

```
public GameObject explosion;
```

In the previous code, we create a placeholder (i.e., a **public** variable) that we will initialize later using drag and drop from the **Inspector** window. This **explosion** object will be used to instantiate an explosion at the point of impact of the projectile.

Now, we just need to create a method that will handle the collision.

- Please add the following code just after the method **Update** (but within the class **CollisionWithProjectile**).

```
void OnCollisionEnter (Collision collision)
{
    if (collision.gameObject.tag == "Player") Destroy (collision.gameObject, 1);

    Instantiate (explosion, transform.position, Quaternion.identity);
}
```

- In the previous code, we use a built-in method called **OnCollisionEnter**. This method is usually called when an object (such as a sphere, a box, or a cylinder) collides with another object. So when this happens, Unity looks for a method spelt exactly this way, and returns information about the collision in the variable **collision**.

Adding Simple AI

> The information about the collision is returned in a variable of type **Collision**, for which we can set the name. In this case, we have called it **collision**, but using a different name (as long as its type is correct) would work just as fine.

- When this collision happens, we just check the tag of the object that we are colliding with; in this case, we look for a tag called **Player** (i.e., we will need to set our third-person controller with this tag so that it is detected accordingly also).

- If this is the case, then we will destroy the object with this tag, and also instantiate an explosion at the position of the projectile (i.e., point of impact).

- Your script should now look like the following:

```
using UnityEngine;
using System.Collections;

public class CollisionWithProjectile : MonoBehaviour
{
    public GameObject explosion;
    // Use this for initialization
    void Start () {

    }

    // Update is called once per frame
    void Update () {

    }

    void OnCollisionEnter (Collision collision)
    {
        if     (collision.gameObject.tag     ==     "Player")     Destroy (collision.gameObject, 1);
            Instantiate (explosion, transform.position, Quaternion.identity);
    }
}
```

- Please save your code.

- Look at the **Console** window and check for any error.

So at this stage, we just need to add this script to the projectile prefab:

- Select the prefab called **projectile**.

- Drag and drop the script that we have just created (i.e., **CollisionWithProjectile**) on this prefab.

- Check that the script is now a component of this prefab by selecting the prefab and looking at its properties in the **Inspector** window, as described on the next figure.

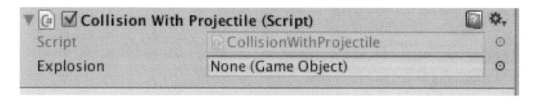

Figure 3-21: Checking that the script is added as a component

Once this done, we just need to specify a type of explosion to be used by this script when a collision occurs between the projectile and another object. For this, we can import and use built-in explosions, which are part of Unity's **Particle** built-in assets.

- Please select: **Assets | Import Package | ParticleSystems**.

- The following window should appear.

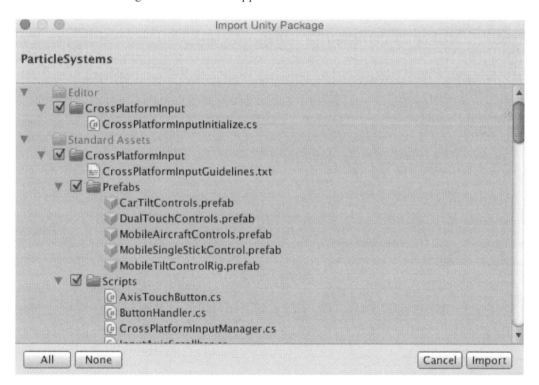

Figure 3-22: Importing the ParticleSystems package (part 1)

Adding Simple AI

- Click the button labeled **Import**, to import all assets included in this package.

- Once the import is complete, a new folder called **ParticleSystems** will be created for these assets in the folder **Standard Assets**, as described in the next figure.

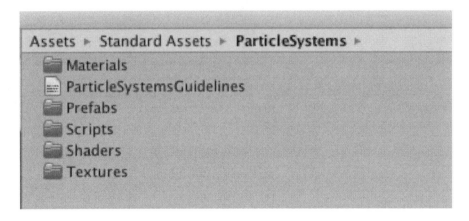

Figure 3-23: Importing the ParticleSystems package (part 2)

At this stage, we can use these new assets so that an explosion can be instantiated at the point of impact.

- Select the object called **ball** in the **Hierarchy** window.

- Check in the **Inspector** that the script **CollisionWithProjectile** is listed as a component for this object.

- Using the **Project** window, navigate to the folder **Assets | Standard Assets | ParticleSystems | Prefabs** and drag and drop the prefab called **explosion** to the field called **explosion** from the script attached to the object called **ball**.

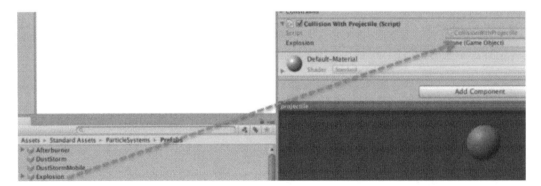

Figure 3-24: Adding a prefab for the explosion (part 1)

[130]

Adding Simple AI

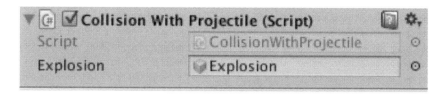

Figure 3-25: Adding a prefab for the explosion (part 2)

- Finally, update the corresponding prefab (i.e., projectile) by clicking on the button labeled Apply located in the top-right corner of the Inspector window. Since this object is used to create the prefab projectile, clicking on Apply will update the prefab also.

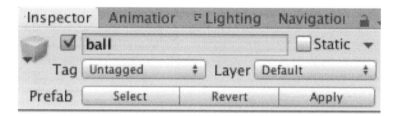

Figure 3-26: Updating the prefab using the Inspector window

Last but not least, so that we can detect collisions with the player, we need to set a tag for the **Third-Person Controller**.

- Select the **Third-Person Controller** from the **Hierarchy** window.

- In the **Inspector** window, you will notice a section called **Tag** just below the name of the object.

Figure 3-27: Creating a tag

- Click on the text **Untagged** and select the option **Player** from the drop-down list, as described on the next figure.

Adding Simple AI

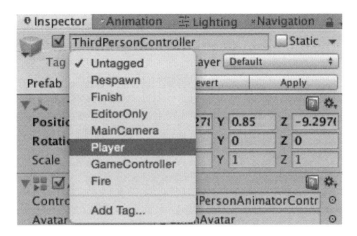

Figure 3-28: Adding a tag for the player

- Play the scene and check that your player disappears once it has been hit by a projectile, and that explosions are instantiated on impact.

FINISHING OUR FIRST GAME

So the game is working fairly well at this stage, the launcher manages to track (and shoot at) the player, and explosions are instantiated upon collision.

There are a few last things that we could do to both improve the game and to be able to reuse the code:

- To be able to reuse the objects that we have created, especially the launcher, it would be great to create a template from them (i.e., a prefab).

- Since the user will lose a life when hit by a projectile, it would be good to keep track of his/her number of lives.

- Finally, it would be nice to create a game with a goal, a scoring system, and the ability to display information onscreen about the status of the game.

So let's make these modifications. First, we will modify the game so that it uses the following gameplay:

- The player needs to collect five objects and reach a platform that symbolizes the end of the level.

- Intelligent launchers will track and shoot at the player.

- There will be four launchers in total.

- The player will avail of safe areas where he/she will be able to hide (away from the projectiles).

- The player, if hit by a projectile, has to restart the level from the starting point.

Please do the following:

- Create four spheres that will be representing the items to be collected by the player. You can rename them **sphere1**, **sphere2**, **sphere3**, and **sphere4**.

- You can then change their position so that their y-coordinate is **1.5**.

- Move them a few meters apart.

Once you have created the spheres, we need to make sure that the player can collect them; we will perform this action by (1) allocating tags to these spheres, (2) then, upon collision, a script linked to the player will detect if the player is colliding with these spheres (i.e., by checking their label), and (3) if this is the case, these spheres will be destroyed.

Adding Simple AI

First, let's create tags for the spheres.

- Select the object **sphere1** in the **Hierarchy** window.

- In the **Inspector** window, you will notice a section called **Tag** just below the name of the object.

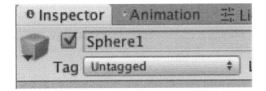

Figure 3-29: Creating a tag

At present, because no tag has been defined or selected for this object, the **Tag** section is set to **Untagged**. So we will create a new tag and allocate it to our object:

- Click on **Untagged**, this will display a list of predefined tags, as well as the option **Add tag...**

- Click on **Add Tag...**, this should display the following window.

Figure 3-30: Creating a new tag

- You may notice that the section **Tags** displays the message **List is Empty**, as we have not defined any new tag yet.

- Click on the + sign to the right of the text **List Empty**, as highlighted on the previous figure.

- Then, enter the name of the new tag, **pick_me**, and press return.

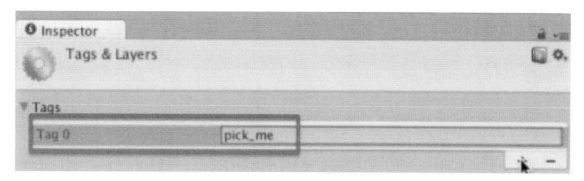

Figure 3-31: Entering the value of the new tag

Now that we have created a new tag, we just need to allocate it to an object:

- In the **Hierarchy** window, select the object **sphere1**.

- In the **Inspector**, go to the **Tag** section; you should now see the tag that you have just created in the drop-down list.

- Select this tag (i.e., click on it once), as described on the next figure.

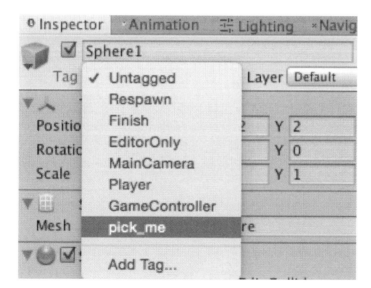

Figure 3-32: Applying a new tag

- You can now apply this tag to the three other spheres, either individually (i.e., by selecting and applying the tag to each sphere one by one, or by selecting all the spheres and applying the tag to all of them in one go).

- At this stage, the tag has been created for each sphere; we could also create a color (e.g., red) and apply it to the spheres so that they are more visible. To do so, you can create a

Adding Simple AI

new **red** material and apply it to the spheres (i.e., select **Create | Material** from the **Project** window and drag and drop this new material to the spheres).

Once this done, we will create a script to detect when the player collides with the objects to be picked-up.

- Please create a new C# script named **CollisionWithPlayer**.

- Open this script and add the following code (new code highlighted in bold) to it.

```
int score;
void Start ()
{
    score = 0;
}
```

- In the previous code, we create a new member variable **score** that will be used to keep track of the score.

- We then initialize the **score** to 0.

We can then add the following code after the **Update** method.

```
void OnCollisionEnter (Collision collision)
{
    if (collision.collider.gameObject.tag == "pick_me")
    {
        Destroy (collision.collider.gameObject);
        score++;
        print ("Score" +score);
    }
}
```

In the previous code:

- We create a new method **OnCollisionEnter**.

- This is a built-in method that is called by Unity every time a collision is detected between the object linked to this script and another object (with a collider).

- Whenever the collision occurs, Unity returns information about the collision using an object of type **Collision**. In our case, this object will be called **collision**.

- If the collision occurs with an object for which the tag is **pick_me**, we then destroy this object and also increase and display the score.

So the full code should look as follows by now:

```csharp
using UnityEngine;
using System.Collections;

public class CollisionWithPlayer : MonoBehaviour {
    // Use this for initialization
    int score;
    void Start ()
    {
        score = 0;
    }
    // Update is called once per frame
    void Update () {
    }
    void OnCollisionEnter (Collision collision)
    {
        print ("Collided with " + collision.collider.gameObject.tag);
        if (collision.collider.gameObject.tag == "pick_me")
        {
            Destroy (collision.collider.gameObject);
            score++;
            print ("Score" +score);
        }
    }
}
```

- Please save your code and ensure that there are no errors.

- Drag and drop this script (i.e., **CollisionWithPlayer**) on the object **ThirdPersonController**.

- Please play the scene and make sure that you can collect the different spheres.

Once this is done, we can then create two platforms: a platform that symbolizes the start of the level, and a platform that symbolizes the end of the level.

Please do the following:

- Create a new cylinder (**GameObject | 3D Object | Cylinder**).

- Set its scale attribute to (**2.0, 0.2, 2.0**) and its **y** position coordinate to **.6**. This is the initial point from where the player will start.

- Rename this object **start**.

- Please repeat the last three steps to create a similar cylinder, but with the name **end** (to speed-up the process, you can duplicate the previous object).

- Place these two cylinders at least 50 meters apart.

[137]

Adding Simple AI

For now, we just need to add three more launchers; for this purpose, we will create a prefab for the launcher and reuse this prefab to create the three additional launchers.

- In the **Project** window, select the folder **launcher**, or any other folder that you have created for the items created in this scene.

- Select the object **launcher** in the **Hierarchy** window.

- Drag and drop this object to the **launcher** folder (or the **Assets** folder).

- This will automatically create a prefab, as illustrated on the next figure.

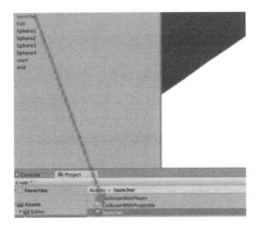

Figure 3-33: Creating a launcher prefab

- Now we can deactivate the **launcher** object that is in the scene.

- Drag and drop the **launcher** prefab on the scene four times to create four launchers.

- This should create four launchers named **launcher (1)**, **launcher (2)**, **launcher (3)**, and **launcher (4)**.

- Include the four launchers between the start and the end of the level.

If you look at the properties of one of these launchers, you may notice that the target is not set, so we will need to do this for all launchers.

- Select all four launchers in the **Hierarchy** window (*using CTRL + click or CTRL + Shift + click*).

- Drag the **ThirdPersonController** from the **Hierarchy** window to the **target** variable for the script **LaunchProjectile** present in the **Inspector** window. Because we have selected the four launchers, the target will be set for these four objects simultaneously.

- So that it is easier to locate the different objects that make up this scene from the y-axis (i.e., from above), you can create two new **Materials** (e.g., blue) and apply these to the launchers (e.g., blue) for the start and end of the level (e.g., green), as illustrated on the next figure.

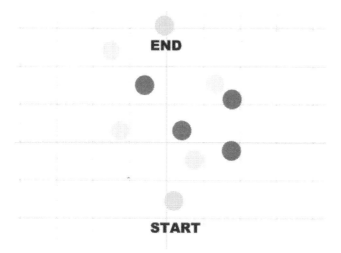

Figure 3-34: Viewing the scene from above

At this stage, all the elements are ready for our game, and we just need to add the following features:

- Make it possible to detect when the player has reached the end of the game.
- Place the player on the starting platform at the beginning of the game or after it has been hit.

Let's do the following:

- Please move the **Third-Person Controller** just 1 meter above the **start** object.

Figure 3-35: Moving the character above the start cylinder

Adding Simple AI

- Open the script **CollisionWithProjectile** and modify it so that, after it has been hit by a projectile, s/he is moved back to the start, as follows (new code highlighted in bold).

```
void OnCollisionEnter (Collision collision)
{
    //if (collision.gameObject.tag == "Player") Destroy (collision.gameObject, 1);
    if (collision.gameObject.tag == "Player")
    {
        collision.gameObject.transform.position = GameObject.Find ("start").transform.position;
    }
    Instantiate (explosion, transform.position, Quaternion.identity);
}
```

In the previous code, we move the player back to the start of the game.

As you play the game you may notice that the explosions may make the game very difficult at the start because every time the projectile explodes, the player is propelled in the air, even if s/he is far from the projectile; you may also notice that the player seems to start way above the starting platform.

To solve the first issue (i.e., the explosions), we can change the type of explosion that is instantiated when a projectile hits an object; we will replace the explosion with smoke instead:

- In the **Project** folder, locate the **projectile** prefab.

- Click on this prefab and look at the **Inspector** window: you should see a component called **CollisionWithProjectile**.

- Click to the right of the variable called **explosion** in the script **CollisionWithProjectile**, as illustrated in the next figure.

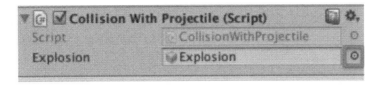

Figure 3-36: Replacing the explosion

This will open a new window where you can specify the prefab to be used for the explosion on impact.

Adding Simple AI

Figure 3-37: Choosing another prefab for the explosion

- In the search window located at the top of this window, please type the word **smoke**; this should narrow down the search to two prefabs.

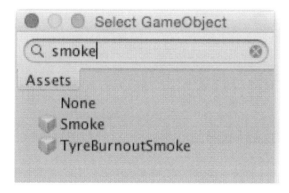

Figure 3-38: Narrowing down the search

- Select the prefab called **Smoke** (double-click on this prefab).
- This should set the explosion with the prefab **Smoke**.

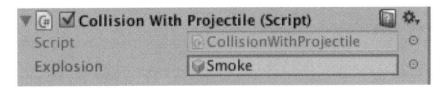

Figure 3-39: Completing the change of prefab for the explosion

Next, we will make sure that the projectile is also destroyed upon collision by modifying the method **OnCollisionEnter** in the script **CollisionWithProjectile** as follows (new code highlighted in bold):

```
Instantiate (explosion, transform.position, Quaternion.identity);
Destroy (gameObject);
```

And last but not least, we will make sure that the smoke lasts only for a few seconds:

- Select the **Smoke** prefab in the project folder (**Assets | Standard Assets | ParticleSystems | Prefabs**).
- In the **Inspector** window, change its **looping** property to **false**.

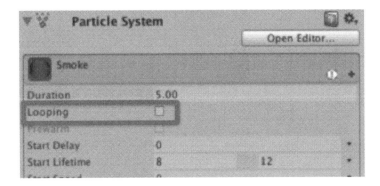

Figure 3-40: Modifying the looping property of the smoke

- Play the scene, and check that the projectiles are destroyed upon impact and also that the smoke disappears after a few seconds.

Finally, we will make sure that the colliders used for each platform (i.e., the start and the end of the game) are correct. At present, as we noticed previously, the player when placed above these, seem to be staying about one meter above its surface, whereas it should be connecting with the top part of the platform.

Adding Simple AI

If we select the start platform and look at its collider, you will notice that a capsule collider is used, which means that the top part of the collider will not follow a flat surface. So we need to change to a more accurate collider that really follows the shape of our cylinder.

- Please right-click on the **start** object in the **Hierarchy** window.

- In the **Inspector**, deactivate the **Capsule Collider** component for this object by unchecking the box to the left of the label **Capsule Collider**.

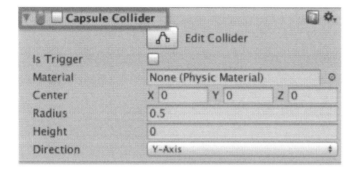

Figure 3-41: Deactivating the capsule collider.

We can now add a new collider, in our case, for increased precision, this will be a mesh collider:

- Click on the button labeled **Add Component** located at the bottom of the **Inspector** window.

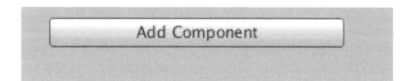

Figure 3-42: Adding a new Collider component

- From the contextual menu, select: **Physics | MeshCollider**.

- Once this is complete, a new mesh collider should be listed as a component of this object.

[143]

Adding Simple AI

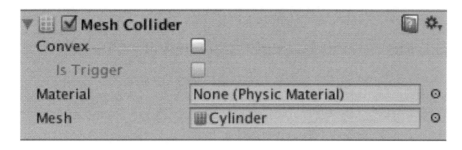

Figure 3-43: The mesh collider listed as a component

- Please repeat the last steps to modify the collider for the object called **end**.
- Play the scene and check that you can jump on both platforms easily.

DETECTING WHEN THE PLAYER HAS REACHED THE END OF THE GAME

At this stage, we need to detect whether the player has reached the end of the level (i.e., the **end** platform) after collecting four objects. So we will need to check for both conditions and then display a message (e.g., "congratulations") when both conditions have been fulfilled. Since we are already counting the number of objects collected, all we need is to access (i.e., read) the score when we have reached the **end** platform.

First, let's detect wen we have reached this platform.

- Open the script **CollisionWithPlayer** and modify it as illustrated in the next code snippet (new code highlighted in bold).

```
void OnCollisionEnter (Collision collision)
{
        if (collision.collider.gameObject.tag == "pick_me")
        {
                Destroy (collision.collider.gameObject);
                score++;
                print ("Score" +score );
        }
        if (collision.collider.gameObject.name == "end" && score == 4)
        {
                print("Congratulations!");
        }
}
```

- In the previous script, we check the name of the object we are colliding with.

- If this is the **end** platform and if the score is **4**, then we print the message "**Congratulations!**", in the **Console** window.

- Please save your code, play the scene, collect four objects, and reach the **end** platform. A message saying "**Congratulations!**" should be displayed in the **Console** window.

Last we will display this message onscreen using **UI** objects. If you are new to **UI** objects, these make it possible to display information (e.g., text, images, menus, buttons, or sliders) onscreen as part of the user interface. So for now, we will be using a **UI Text** object.

- Create a new **UI Text** object (**GameObject | UI | Text**).

- Rename this object **message**.

- Select this object.

Adding Simple AI

Modify its properties in the **Inspector** as follows:

- PosX:0
- PosY:0
- PosZ:0
- Width: 500
- Height: 200
- Font Size: 40
- Vertical alignment: middle
- Horizontal alignment: middle
- Color: green (or any color of your choice)

We can then modify the script **CollisionWithPlayer** so that it displays a message when all spheres have been collected.

- Modify the script **CollisionWithPlayer** as follows:

```
using UnityEngine;
using System.Collections;
using UnityEngine.UI;

public class CollisionWithPlayer : MonoBehaviour {

    // Use this for initialization
    int score;
    void Start ()
    {
        score = 0;
        GameObject.Find("message").GetComponent<Text>().text ="";
    }
```

In the previous code:

- The third line introduces the name space **UnityEngine.UI**. This may be new to you, so let me explain. The **Text UI** elements are part of a sub-library called **UI**, which is part of the library **UnityEngine**. So, if we want to refer to the **Text UI** element, we can use **GetComponent <Text>** instead, and Unity will look into the library **UnityEngine.UI** to find the **UI Text** component.

- Then we specify that the text for the object called message is set to a blank string; in other words, we initialize the text field so that no message is displayed until we reach the end platform.

We can then display the message when the player has reached the **end** platform by modifying the code in the **Update** method, in the script **CollisionWithPlayer**, as follows (new code highlighted in bold).

```
if (collision.collider.gameObject.name == "end" && score >= 2)
{
        print("Congratulations!!!");
        GameObject.Find("message").GetComponent<Text>().text = "Congratulations!";
}
```

In the previous code, we change the message, as we have done before, but this time with the string "**Congratulations**".

LEVEL ROUNDUP

Well this is it!

In this chapter, we have learned about instantiating objects in C#. We have created a very simply AI-driven launcher that follows the player and shoots projectile in his/her direction, and at a controlled rate. We also managed to create explosions upon collision. Finally, we created a scoring system and a mini-game whereby the player has to collect four objects, and also avoid the projectiles, before reaching the end of the level. So yes, we have made some considerable progress, and we have by now looked at some simple ways to implement artificial intelligence in our games.

Checklist

You can consider moving to the next chapter if you can do the following:

- Create prefabs.
- Instantiate prefabs.
- Add **Rigidbody** components.
- Shoot projectiles (i.e., apply a force to an object with a Rigidbody component from a script).
- Understand why and how to cast variables.
- Display messages onscreen.

Adding Simple AI

Quiz

It's now time to check your knowledge with a quiz. So please try to answer the following questions. The solutions are included in your resource pack. Good luck!

1. The method **onControllerColliderHit** is called whenever a collision occurs between the **ThirdPersonController** and anther object that includes a collider.

2. To be able to access a variable from a script through the **Inspector**, this variable has to be declared as **public** in the script.

3. Write the missing line in this code to be able to destroy the object we have collided with.

```
function OnCollisionEnter (Collision collision)
{
<MISSING LINE>
}
```

4. There is only one way to create a prefab in Unity, that is through the menu **Create | Prefab**.

5. A mesh collider will detect collision more precisely than a capsule collider when applied to a spherical object.

6. Find one error in the following code.

```
void Start ()
{
    score = 0;
    GameObject.Find("message").GetComponent<UIText>().text    ="";
}
```

7. Any object selected in the **Hierarchy** window can be duplicated using the shortcut *CTRL + D*.

8. If the object attached to the next script has a **Rigidbody** component, the following code will access this component and apply a forward force to it.

```
gameObject.GetComponent<Rigidbody>().AddForce(transform.forward * 1000);
```

9. Explosions prefabs need to be imported using the **ParticleSystems** asset, in order to be used in Unity.

10. If the following error message appears "**Cannot implicitly convert type**", what do you need to do with the following code:

```
GameObject   t   =   Instantiate   (projectile,   transform.position, Quaternion.identity);
```

  a) Make sure that the type of the variable to the left of the = sign is the same as the type of the variable on right of the = sign.
  b) Cast the variable to the right of the = sign using **(GameObject)**.

[149]

c) All of the above.

Adding Simple AI

Solutions to the Quiz

1. FALSE (it should be **On**ControllerColliderHit).

2. TRUE.

3.
```
function OnCollisionEnter (Collision collision)
{
Destroy (collision.collider.gameObject;
}
```

4. FALSE.

5. TRUE.

6.
```
void Start ()
{
    score = 0;
    //GameObject.Find("message").GetComponent<UIText>().text     ="";
    //should be
    GameObject.Find("message").GetComponent<UI.Text>().text     ="";
    OR
    GameObject.Find("message").GetComponent< Text>().text ="";
}
```

7. TRUE.

8. TRUE.
```
gameObject.GetComponent<Rigidbody>().AddForce(transform.forward * 1000);
```

9. TRUE.

10. c (all the above)

[151]

Adding Simple AI

Challenge 1

Now that you have managed to complete this chapter and that you have improved your skills, let's modify the game to add more interaction.

- Change the onscreen message to "**You have collected an object**" every time the user has collected an object.

- Display the score onscreen (i.e., create a new **UI Text** object and access it whenever the score is updated).

- Create a timer so that this message is displayed only for 5 seconds.

Challenge 2

It is now time to try to use different prefabs:

- Look into the **ParticleSystems** assets folder and look at the different types of prefabs available.

- Successively use two different prefabs from this folder for when the ball hits an object.

- Experiment with the other prefabs and add them to the scene (e.g., steam or dust storm).

4
CREATING AND MANAGING WEAPONS

In this section we will discover how to create and manage weapons using a simple inventory system.

After completing this chapter, you will be able to:

- Create different weapons including a gun, an automatic gun, and a grenade launcher.
- Collect and manage ammunitions.
- Switch between weapons.
- Aim at targets using ray casting and a crosshair.
- Detect objects in the distance based on the crosshair.
- Simulate the impact of a bullet using particles.

Creating and Managing Weapons

In this section, we will be creating a training camp with the following features:

- The player will avail of three different weapons.
- The player will need to hit specific targets.
- The player will be able to collect ammunitions when needed.

SETTING-UP THE ENVIRONMENT

In this section we will create a very simple environment for this training camp.

So let's get started:

- Save the previous scene (**File | Save Scene**).

- Create a new scene (**File | New Scene**).

- Rename this scene **training-camp** or any other name of your choice using **File | Save Scene**.

- You may also create a new folder to store assets created in this scene (i.e., select **Create | Folder** from the **Project** window).

- Change the light settings so that the ambient light is brighter (**Window | Lighting**).

We will now create a simple ground and three targets.

- Create a new cube and rename it **ground**.

- Change its position to **(0, 0, 0)** and its scale properties to **(100, 1, 100)**.

- You can apply a texture to the ground by choosing one of the textures present in the resource pack (e.g., ground).

If you import a texture to be used in Unity, please make sure that its **Texture Type** property (available from the **Inspector** window, as illustrated in the next figure) is set to **Texture**. To do so you can select the texture imported, set its type to **Texture** in the **Inspector** window, and then click on the button Apply located in the bottom-right corner of the **Inspector** window. If this texture is to be repeated several times (i.e., tiled) over the surface of an object, you may also set the option **Wrap Mode** to **Repeat**.

Figure 4-1: Setting the Texture Type attribute of an imported texture

We will now create three targets that will be used for the training:

- Create a new **Cube**.

- Rename this cube **target1**.

- Using the **Rect** tool and/or the **Move** tool, rescale the cube on the y-axis so that its **position** is **(0,4,0)** and its **scale** property **(1, 6.5, 1)**. At this stage, what really matters is that this target can be seen (and targeted) easily.

- You can also paint this target in red by either applying an existing material that you have created in the previous scene, or by creating a new color material for this scene (i.e., select **Create | Material** from the **Project** window, change the color of the material and drag and drop it on the target).

- We can now duplicate this target three times, to add three identical targets. You can rename these targets **target2**, **target3**, and **target4**.

- Move these targets apart, so that they are aligned and about three meters apart; for example, they could be at the positions **(3, 4, 0)**, **(6, 4, 0)** and **(9, 4, 0)**.

So at this stage we have four targets that are aligned; we will now just add a First-Person Controller to the scene:

- Navigate to the folder **Assets | Standard Assets | Characters | FirstPersonCharacter | Prefabs**.

- Drag and drop the prefab **FPSController** to the scene, and make sure that it is just above the ground.

- This controller will be used to navigate through the scene.

- We can deactivate the object **MainCamera** so that only the camera embedded on the First-Person Controller is used.

- Play the scene (*CTRL + P*) and check that you can walk around the scene.

DETECTING OBJECTS AHEAD USING RAYCASTING

At this stage, we would like to detect what is in front of the player so that when we use our weapon (e.g., gun), we know whether an object is in the line of fire before shooting. To do so, we will use ray casting. So we will create some code to be able to detect what is in front of the player using a ray.

A ray is a bit like a laser beam; it is casted over a distance and usually employed to detect if an object is in the line of fire. In our case, we will cast a ray from the player (forward) and detect if it "collides" with another object. Before we do this, we can also use a ray in debug mode (i.e., only visible in the scene view), just to check its direction and length.

Rays can be used for many applications, from weapons to controlling objects (e.g., opening a door only if you are facing it rather than using collision).

The first ray that we will create will be used for testing purposes; it will only be visible in the scene view for the time being and will help us to gauge whether the ray casting technique used for collision detection will be successful.

- Please create a new script called **ManageWeapons**.
- Open this script and modify it as illustrated below.

```
public class ManageWeapons : MonoBehaviour
{
    Camera playersCamera;
    Ray rayFromPlayer;
    // Use this for initialization
    void Start ()
    {
        playersCamera = GetComponent<Camera>();
    }

    // Update is called once per frame
    void Update ()
    {

    }
}
```

In the previous code:

- We declare a new **GameObject** called **playersCamera**. This camera will be used for ray casting.

Creating and Managing Weapons

- We also declare a new ray called **rayFromPlayer** that will also be used for our ray casting.

- In the method **Start**, this camera is then initialized with the camera that is linked to the First-Person Controller.

> Since the game, in this scene, will be using a First-Person view, the scene will be viewed through the eyes of the player; so we will cast a ray as if it was originating from the eyes of the player; since the scene is rendered through the camera attached to the First-Person controller, we will cast a ray from the middle of this lens (or the screen) and forward.

- You may just check that there is a camera attached to the **First-Person Controller** using the **Inspector** window: if you click on the object **FPSController**, you will see an object within called **FirstPersonCharacter**. If you click on this object (i.e., **FirstPersonCharacter**), and look at the **Inspector** window, you will see that, amongst other things, it includes a camera component.

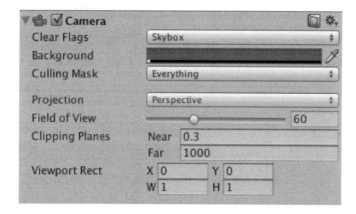

Figure 4-2: Checking the camera for the FPC

> So again, this camera is linked to the object **FirstPersonCharacter** (and not the **FPSController**); this is really important because the script will be linked to the latter. If you were to add this script to the object **FPSController** instead, an error would occur because this object does not have a camera component.

- Let's further modify this script as follows.

Creating and Managing Weapons

```
void Update ()
{
    rayFromPlayer = playersCamera.ScreenPointToRay (new Vector3
(Screen.width/2, Screen.height/2, 0));
    Debug.DrawRay(rayFromPlayer.origin, rayFromPlayer.direction * 100,
Color.red);

}
```

In the previous code, we do the following:

- We initialize our ray defined earlier; this ray will be originating from the camera used for the **First-Person Controller**, from the centre of the screen, which is defined by the x and y coordinates **Screen.width/2** (i.e., half the screen's width) and **Screen.height/2** (i.e., half the screen's height); the z coordinate is ignored. So at this stage, we know where the ray will start. By default, the ray will point outward.

- On the next line, we use the static method **DrawRay** and specify three parameters: the origin of the ray, its direction, and its color. By using **ray.origin** we will start the ray from the middle of the screen. By using **rayFromPlayer.direction*100**, we specify that the ray's length is 100 meters.

We are now ready to use this script:

- Please save your code and check that there are no errors left.

- Drag and drop the script form the **Project** window to the object **FirstPersonCharater** (the one within the object **FPSController**).

- Change the layout of your scene so that you can see both the **Scene** and the **Game** view simultaneously (e.g., drag the **Scene** view to the right of the **Console** tab).

- Play the scene.

- Check that you can see a ray casted from the camera of the FPS Controller, as described on the next figure.

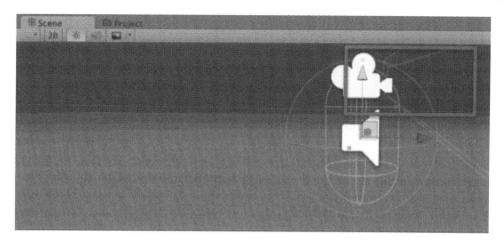

Figure 4-3: Casting a ray using the debug mode

Once this done, we can now apply a real ray casting method, by using a ray that will point in the exact same direction, but that will, in addition, detect any objects ahead of the player. To be more accurate the new ray will detect any collider attached to an object in front of the player.

- Please open the script **ManageWeapons**, and modify it as follows (new code highlighted in bold).

```
public class ManageWeapons : MonoBehaviour
{
    Camera playersCamera;
    Ray rayFromPlayer;
    RaycastHit hit;
```

In the previous code, we declare an object of type **RaycastHit**; this object will be used to store information about the collision between the ray casted from the player (i.e., from its camera), and the object in front of the player.

- We will then modify the **Update** method to cast the ray and detect any object in sight (the new code highlighted in bold):

```
void Update ()
{
        rayFromPlayer    =    playersCamera.ScreenPointToRay    (new    Vector3
(Screen.width/2, Screen.height/2, 1000));
        Debug.DrawRay(rayFromPlayer.origin,    rayFromPlayer.direction    *    100 ,
Color.red);
        if (Physics.Raycast(rayFromPlayer, out hit, 100))
        {
                print (" The object " + hit.collider.gameObject.name +" is in front of
the player");
        }
}
```

In the previous code:

- We cast a ray using the keyword **Physics.RayCast**; the method **RayCast** takes three parameters: the ray (**rayFromPlayer**), an object where the information linked to the collision between the ray and another collider is stored (**hit**), and the length of the ray (**100**). The keyword **out** is used so that the information returned about the collision is easily accessible (as a reference rather than a structure; this is comparable to a type conversion or casting).

- If this ray hits an object (i.e., its collider), we print a message that displays the name of this object. To obtain this name, we access the collider involved in the collision, then the corresponding **GameObject** using **hit.collider.gameObject.name**.

- Please play the scene, and as you walk towards one of the targets, for example **target1**, the message "**target1 is in front of the player** " should be displayed in the **Console** window.

The method **Debug.DrawRay** will create a ray that we can see in the scene view and that can be used for debugging purposes to check that a ray effectively points in the right direction; however, **Debug.DrawRay** does not detect collisions with objects. So while it is useful to check the direction of a particular ray in the **Scene** view, this ray needs to be combined to a different method to be able to detect collisions; one of these methods is called **Physics.Raycast**.

CREATING A WEAPON

So, well done: at this stage we can cast rays and detect the object in front of the player. So the next step for us is to create and fire a weapon, and detect, using the ray cast, whether and where the bullet has hit a target. In this case, we will instantiate particles at the exact point of impact. So let's open the script **ManageWeapons**.

First, we will define a placeholder (i.e., a **public** variable accessible from the **Inspector**) that holds the particles to be used at the point of impact (i.e., at the intersection between the ray and the object in front of the player).

- Please modify the code to declare a new **GameObject** as follows (new code in bold).

```
public class ManageWeapons : MonoBehaviour
{
    Camera playersCamera;
    Ray rayFromPlayer;
    RaycastHit hit;
    public GameObject sparksAtImpact;
```

- We will then make sure that the ray is casted only when a specific key has been pressed, by adding the following code to the **Update** method (new code highlighted in bold).

```
Debug.DrawRay(rayFromPlayer.origin, rayFromPlayer.direction * 100, Color.red);
if (Input.GetKeyDown(KeyCode.F))
{
    if (Physics.Raycast(rayFromPlayer, out hit, 100))
    {
        print (" The object " + hit.collider.gameObject.name +" is in front of the player");
        Vector3 positionOfImpact;
        positionOfImpact = hit.point;
        Instantiate (sparksAtImpact, positionOfImpact, Quaternion.identity);
    }
}
```

In the previous code,

- We check that the key **F** has been pressed (you could have chosen any other key also) before ray casting.

- We then create a new **Vector3** variable called **positionOfImpact** that is used to store the position of the impact (i.e., this is the intersection between the ray and the object in front of the player).

Creating and Managing Weapons

- We initialize this variable with the position of impact; this position is found using the variable **hit.point**.

- We then instantiate a new **GameObject** (i.e., **sparkAtImpact**) at this exact position.

The last thing we need to do is to set the variable for the particles to be emitted on impact (**sparkAtImpact**). We can do this, as we have done before, using the **Inspector**.

- Please select the object **FirstPersonCharacter** (i.e., the object within the object **FPSController**).

- In the **Inspector** window, in the section called **ManageWeapons** for this object, click on the small circle to the right of the variable **SparksAtImpact**, as described on the next figure.

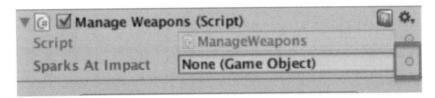

Figure 4-4: Adding a new particle effect on impact (part 1)

- Once this is done, a new window will appear where you can perform a search.

- Search for the term **smoke**, using the search field: this should return, amongst other prefabs, the prefab called **Smoke**.

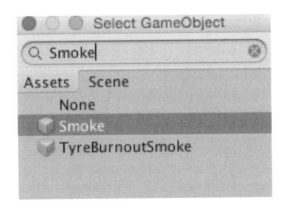

Figure 4-5: Adding a new particle effect on impact (part 2)

- Double click on the prefab called **Smoke** to select it.

- Once this is done, the **Inspector** should now list this prefab for the variable **SparksAtImpact**.

Creating and Managing Weapons

Figure 4-6: Adding a new particle effect on impact (part 3)

Once this is done, there is a last thing we can do to make shooting more accurate: adding a crosshair.

- Import the **crosshair** image from the resource pack to your project.
- Create a new **RawImage** Object (**Game Object | UI | RawImage**).
- Using the **Inspector** window, change its position to **(0, 0, 0)** so that it is displayed in the center of the screen.

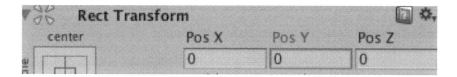

Figure 4-7: Positioning the crosshair

And finally, set its texture in the section **RawImage**, by dragging and dropping the **crosshair** texture from your **Project** window (i.e., where you have imported this texture) to the variable **Texture**.

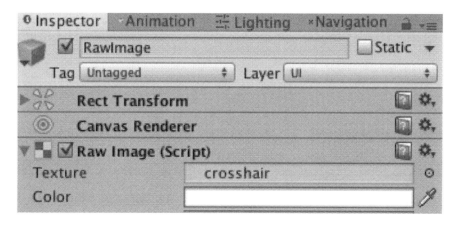

Figure 4-8: Adding the crosshair texture

[165]

Creating and Managing Weapons

- We could also rename this object **crosshair**, using the **Hierarchy** or the **Inspector** window.

- Once this is done, the **Game** view should look as follows:

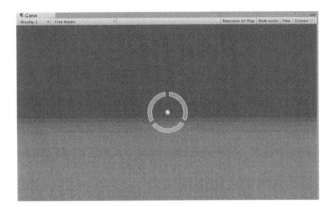

Figure 4-9: Displaying the crosshair

- Now, we can play the scene, and use the crosshair to aim at the different targets.

- As you press the **F** key, you should see that smoke is created at the point of impact.

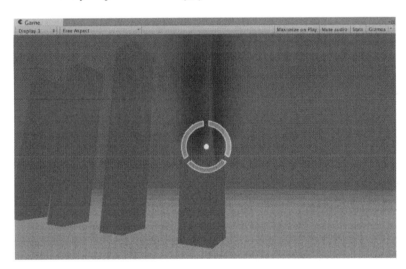

Figure 4-10: Shooting at a target.

Last but not list, we will try to manage ammunitions for this particular gun. You see, at present, the player can shoot indefinitely; so we could just give the player an initial amount of bullets, and make it possible to fire the gun only if there are bullets left.

- Please modify the start of the script as follows (new code in bold).

Creating and Managing Weapons

```
public class ManageWeapons : MonoBehaviour
{
    Camera playersCamera;
    Ray rayFromPlayer;
    RaycastHit hit;
    public GameObject sparksAtImpact;
    private int gunAmmo = 3;
```

In the previous code, we declare a new variable that will be used to store the number of ammunitions left.

- Then, we can modify the code to manage these ammunitions, as follows (new code in bold):

```
if (Input.GetKeyDown(KeyCode.F) && gunAmmo > 0)
{
    if (Physics.Raycast(rayFromPlayer, out hit, 100))
    {
        print (" The object " + hit.collider.gameObject.name +" is in front of the player");
        Vector3 positionOfImpact;
        positionOfImpact = hit.point;
        Instantiate   (sparksAtImpact,   positionOfImpact, Quaternion.identity);

    }
    gunAmmo --;
    print ("You have "+gunAmmo + " bullets left");
```

In the previous code:

- We check that we have enough ammunition before firing the gun.
- If this is the case, we decrease the number of bullets left.
- We then display the number of bullets left.

Please play the scene, and check that after shooting three times, you can no longer fire the gun.

MANAGING DAMAGE

So at this stage, we have managed to create a weapon and fire bullets precisely using ray casting and a crosshair. This being said, it would be great to be able to manage the targets (that we will refer to as NPCs in this section) by knowing how many times they have been hit and when they should be destroyed (e.g., after being hit three times). So for this purpose, we will create a script that will store the NPC's health, count how many times it was hit, decrease its health whenever it has been hit, and destroy it after its health has reached 0.

So let's create our script.

- Please create a new C# script and rename it **ManageNPC**.

- Add the following code (new code in bold).

```
public class ManageNPC : MonoBehaviour
{
    private int health;
    public GameObject smoke;
    void Start ()
    {
        health = 100;
    }
    public void gotHit()
    {
        health -=50;
    }
```

In the previous code:

- We declare two variables: **health** and **smoke**; the former is used to track the NPCs' health, and the latter is used so that we can instantiate particles (e.g., explosions) when and where the NPC has been destroyed.

- We then initialize the health to 100 in the **Start** function.

We also create a method **gotHit** that is declared as **public**. This means that it will be accessible from outside this script. This method will be called whenever the object has been hit; when this happens, the health is decreased by **50**.

- Please add the next code to the script (i.e., within the class **ManageNPC**; new code in bold).

```
public void Destroy()
{

    GameObject lastSmoke = (GameObject) (Instantiate (smoke, transform.position, Quaternion.identity));
    Destroy (lastSmoke,3);
    Destroy(gameObject);

}
void Update ()
{
    if (health <=0) Destroy();
}
```

In the previous code:

- In the method **Update**, we check the status of the health. If the health is **0** or less, then we call the method **Destroy**.

- In the method **Destroy**, we instantiate a **GameObject** (e.g., smoke) at the position of the NPC.

- We then destroy the smoke after 3 seconds and we also destroy the NPC.

Once these changes have been made, we can:

- Save the script.

- Drag and drop this script on all targets.

- Set the variable **smoke** for the script embedded on these targets with a particle effect of your choice (e.g., smoke) by dragging and dropping a prefab of your choice on the variable called **smoke,** for the script **ManageNPC** linked to each target, using the **Inspector**.

Once this is done, we just need to modify the script **ManageWeapons** so that we can modify the health of each NPC when it has been hit:

- Please open the script **ManageWeapons**.

- Modify the code as follows (new code in bold).

```
if (Physics.Raycast(rayFromPlayer, out hit, 100))
{
        print (" The object " + hit.collider.gameObject.name +" is in front of the player");
        Vector3 positionOfImpact;
        positionOfImpact = hit.point;
        Instantiate (sparksAtImpact, positionOfImpact, Quaternion.identity);
        GameObject objectTargeted;
        if (hit.collider.gameObject.tag == "target")
        {
                objectTargeted = hit.collider.gameObject;
                objectTargeted.GetComponent<ManageNPC>().gotHit();
        }
}
```

In the previous code:

- We create a new **GameObject** called **objectTargeted**.
- We then set this object with the object that is in the line of sight.
- If the tag of this object is **target** we will access its script called **ManageNPC** and call (or evoke) the method **gotHit**.

The last things we need to do is to create a tag called **target** (using the **Inspector**, as we have done before) and apply it to all the targets. We can also set the initial number of bullets, **gunAmmo**, to **10** (instead of three, in the script **ManageWeapons**) so that we can test the game properly.

- Please make these changes (i.e., add the tag target to all targets and set the initial number of ammos to 10).
- Please play the scene.
- Shoot at each target twice and check that they disappear, and that smoke has been created at their previous location.

COLLECTING AND MANAGING AMMUNITIONS

At this stage, the game level is working well, however our player may run out of ammunitions. So it would be good to create ammunitions that can be collected by the player. To do so, we will create and texture boxes that will be used as ammunitions; we will also give them a label, and detect whenever the player collides with them. We will also get to create prefabs with these so that they can be reused later (i.e., in different levels).

So let's create these ammunition boxes:

- Please create a new cube.

- Move it slightly away from the targets and above the ground, for example at the position (1.0, 1.5, 10.0).

- Use a texture of your choice or import a texture from the resource pack and apply it to the box.

- Create a new tag called **ammo_gun** and apply it to this cube.

Once this is done, we just need to detect collisions between this cube and the player, and increase the player's ammunitions accordingly. This being said, collision detection would usually be handled by the **FPSController** object rather than the **FirstPersonCharacter** object; this is because the **FPSController** object already has a collider whereas the **FirstPersonController** object doesn't have any; as a result, we could proceed in at list two ways:

(1) We could create a new script, attach it to the **FPSController**, and also copy (or transfer) all the code that we have created to date to this script; this would involve some minor to medium changes, but it would have the benefit of having all our code for the weapon and collision management associated to the player in only one script

OR

(2) We could just create a new script, to be attached to the **FirstPersonCharacter**, that detects collision and that notifies our already existing script (**ManageWeapons**) of the collision. This would only involve one line of code, and very minor changes.

So, with all of this considered, we could apply the second solution. However, bear in mind that we could have solved this challenge in many other ways.

So we will create a mechanism whereby:

- A script attached to the **FPSController** will detect collisions.

- It will then notify the script **ManageWeapons** of a collision and pass information related to this collision.

So let's get started:

- Please create a new script called **ManageCollisionWithPlayer**.

- Add the following code to this script, within the class **ManageCollisionWithPlayer**.

[171]

Creating and Managing Weapons

```
void OnControllerColliderHit (ControllerColliderHit hit)
{
transform.GetChild(0).GetComponent<ManageWeapons>().manageCollisions(hit);
}
```

In the previous code:

- We use the built-in method **OnControllerColliderHit**; this method is called whenever a collision is detected between the **FPSController** and another object.

- The information about the collision is returned in an object of type **ControllerColliderHit**.

- We name this object **hit**, and then pass it to the script **ManageWeapons** through a member method (that we yet have to create) called **manageCollisions**.

- This method is accessed using the syntax **transform.getChild**; this means that we access the first child of the object **FPSController** (i.e., the first and only child here). Again, this is due to the hierarchy of our game whereby the object **FirstPersonCharacter** is a child of the object **FPSController**.

- Please save your code, check for any error in the **Console** window.

Once this done, we can save this script and modify the script **ManageWeapons**, to add a new method within the class, as follows:

```
public void manageCollisions (ControllerColliderHit hit)
{
        print ("Collided with " + hit.collider.gameObject.name);
        if (hit.collider.gameObject.tag =="ammo_gun")
        {
            gunAmmo +=5;
            if (gunAmmo > 10) gunAmmo = 10;
            Destroy (hit.collider.gameObject);
        }
}
```

In the previous code:

- We declare a new method called **manageCollisions**. This method takes one parameter of type **ControllerColliderHit**.

- We then print the name of the object we have collided with.

- We check if we have collided with gun ammunitions.

- If this is the case, we increase the ammunitions for the player by **5**.

- We then check if we have reached the maximum number of ammos that we can carry.

- If this is the case, we cap the number of ammunitions to this maximum.
- We then destroy the ammo pack.

Please save your code, check for any errors in the **Console** window; then drag and drop the script **ManageCollisionWithPlayer** from the **Project** window on the object called **FPSController** located in the **Inspector** window (or the **Scene** view).

You can now play the scene. As you play the scene, please check that you can shoot at the targets several times, that you can collect some ammos, and also that your ammunition levels have been updated accordingly.

BUILDING A WEAPON MANAGEMENT SYSTEM WITH ARRAYS

At present, we have a relatively simple weapon management system that works with one weapon. We can collect ammos and also shoot at targets. However, in the next sections, we will be adding more types of weapons (i.e., automatic gun and grenade), so we need to find a way to manage these simply, using structures that make it easy to track the ammunitions for each of them or the time it takes to reload a weapon. So, before even creating new weapons, we will make sure that we have a structure in place that will make it possible to track the following information, for each of them:

- Whether the player has this weapon.

- The reload time for this weapon.

- The name of the weapon.

- The ammunitions that the player is carrying (or currently has) for this weapon.

- The maximum number of ammunitions that the player can carry for this weapon.

To do so, we will be using a combination of arrays and constant variables. The process will be as follows.

- We will create an array for each of the variables that are common across the weapons: an array for the weapons' name, an array for their reload time, an array to check whether the player has this weapon, an array for the corresponding ammunitions, and an array for the maximum number of ammunitions that can be carried for this weapon.

- We will then create an index for each of these weapons; for example, a gun could be referred as index 0, the automatic gun could be referred as index 1, and the grenade launcher could be referred as index 2. These indexes will be used to access information in the arrays for a particular weapon.

- Whenever the player presses the tab key, we will switch between the active weapons (i.e., the one that the player is carrying).

- When the player presses the **F** key, we check that there is enough ammunition for the current weapons, and then, if this is the case, we fire this particular weapon.

- As the player tries to shoot another time, we check the reload time for this particular weapon (e.g., 2 for a normal gun, .5 for an automatic gun, etc.).

- When we collect an ammo pack, we check its type, and also update the ammunition levels for the weapon that we currently carry.

So, this is the general principle; now that it is clearer, let's implement the corresponding code.

Please open the script **ManageWeapons**, and add the following code at the beginning of the class (new code in bold).

```
public class ManageWeapons : MonoBehaviour
{
    private const int WEAPON_GUN = 0;
    private const int WEAPON_AUTO_GUN = 1;
    private const int WEAPON_GRENADE = 2;

    private int activeWeapon = WEAPON_GUN;
    private float timer;
    private bool timerStarted;
    private bool canShoot = true;
    private int currentWeapon;

    private bool [] hasWeapon;
    private int [] ammos;
    private int [] maxAmmos;
    private float [] reloadTime;
    private string [] weaponName;
```

In the previous code:

- We first declare a set of three constant variables, **WEAPON_GUN**, **WEAPON_AUTO_GUN**, and **WEAPON_GRENADE**. These variables are constant, so their value will always be the same.

- We then declare four other variables: **activeWeapon**, **timer** (this will be used to simulate the reload time), **timerStarted** (this will be used to check whether the reload has started), **canShoot** (this will be used to check if the player can shoot or whether the reload time has elapsed).

- Finally we also declare five arrays that will share common properties across weapons including: whether the player has this weapon (**hasWeapon**), the number of ammos for a particular weapon (**ammos**), the maximum number of ammos for this weapon (**maxAmmos**), the reload time (**reloadTime**), and the name of this weapon (**weaponName**).

Now, we just need to initialize these variables; so let's add the following code to the **Start** function:

Creating and Managing Weapons

```
void Start ()
{
    ammos = new int [3];
    hasWeapon = new bool [3];
    maxAmmos = new int [3];
    reloadTime = new float [3];
    weaponName = new string [3];
```

In the previous code, we initialize all the arrays that we have declared previously; they are initialized using the syntax **new dataType [size]**. Because we only plan on having three different weapons for now, we set a size of 3 for all these arrays.

> Note that each element of the arrays will be accessible using the syntax **arrayName [index]**; for example the first element of the array **ammos** will be accessible using **ammos [0]**; for each array, the first element starts at **0**, so the last element will be, in our case, at the index **2** (i.e., the size of the array minus 1). Although you can also initialize an array without specifying its size, it is good practice to set its size at the beginning if we know that it will not change overtime.

> Also note that many of the errors related to the use of arrays are often linked to their size. For example, you may try to access an array element at the index 7, whereas the size of the array is 5; in this case Unity may display a message telling your that you are "**out of bounds**" which means that you are trying to access an element that is outside the bounds of this array. We will look into these types of errors later but this is something to keep in mind.

After initializing the arrays we can initialize some of values in these arrays; please add the following code to the **Start** method (after the previous code):

```
hasWeapon [WEAPON_GUN] = true;
hasWeapon [WEAPON_AUTO_GUN] = false;
hasWeapon [WEAPON_GRENADE] = false;

weaponName[WEAPON_GUN] = "GUN";
weaponName[WEAPON_AUTO_GUN] = "AUTOMATIC GUN";
weaponName[WEAPON_GRENADE] = "GRENADE";

ammos [WEAPON_GUN] = 10;
ammos [WEAPON_AUTO_GUN] = 0;
ammos [WEAPON_GRENADE] = 0;


maxAmmos [WEAPON_GUN] = 20;
maxAmmos [WEAPON_AUTO_GUN] = 20;
maxAmmos [WEAPON_GRENADE] = 5;


currentWeapon = WEAPON_GUN;
```

In the previous code:

- We first set the content of the array **hasWeapon**. For each element of the array, we use the constant variables defined earlier. So the first element of the array (index 0), is referred to using the constant variable **WEAPON_GUN**, the second element (1) is referred to using the constant variable **WEAPON_GUN_AUTO_GUN**, and so on. Using these notations, we set the elements of the array **hasweapon** to specify that we initially only have a gun.

- Then, using the same principle, we initialize the values for the array **ammos** (i.e., 10 ammos for the gun, and no ammos for the other weapons), **maxAmmos** (i.e., 20 ammos for the gun and the automatic gun, and 5 grenades).

- Finally we specify that the current weapon is the gun.

Once this is done, we need to find a system that switches between the weapons that we have whenever we press the *Tab* key on the keyboard; so the following method will be used:

- Pressing the tab key will change the index of the current weapon (0 for gun, 1 for the automatic gun, or 2 for grenades).

- If we have only one weapon, then pressing the Tab key will not cause any change.

- If we have the three weapons, pressing the tab key will select the gun, the automatic gun, or the grenades.

- If we have two weapons, pressing the tab key will toggle between these two weapons.

Creating and Managing Weapons

Let's type the corresponding code; please add the following code to the **Update** method (just before the end of this method) in the script **ManageWeapons**:

```
if (Input.GetKeyDown(KeyCode.Tab))
{
        if     (hasWeapon[WEAPON_GUN]      &&      hasWeapon[WEAPON_AUTO_GUN]      &&
hasWeapon[WEAPON_GRENADE])
        {
                currentWeapon++;
                if (currentWeapon>2) currentWeapon = 0;
        }
        else if (hasWeapon[WEAPON_GUN] && hasWeapon[WEAPON_AUTO_GUN])
        {
                if (currentWeapon == WEAPON_GUN) currentWeapon = WEAPON_AUTO_GUN;
                else currentWeapon = WEAPON_GUN;
        }
        else if (hasWeapon[WEAPON_GUN] && hasWeapon[WEAPON_GRENADE])
        {
                if (currentWeapon == WEAPON_GUN) currentWeapon = WEAPON_GRENADE;
                else currentWeapon = WEAPON_GUN;
         }
        else if (hasWeapon[WEAPON_AUTO_GUN] && hasWeapon[WEAPON_GRENADE])
        {
                if    (currentWeapon     ==    WEAPON_AUTO_GUN)    currentWeapon    =
WEAPON_GRENADE;
                else currentWeapon = WEAPON_AUTO_GUN;
        }
        else
        {
        }
        print    ("Current     Weapon:     "+    weaponName[currentWeapon]     +
"("+ammos[currentWeapon]+")");
}
```

In the previous code:

- We first check whether the **Tab** key has been pressed.

- If this is the case, we check how many and what types of weapons the player currently has.

- In the case of three weapons, we increase the index of the current weapon; if this count is more that 2 (remember that the index starts at 0 so the third item would be at the index 2) then it is set to 1; this way we can loop through the three weapons (i.e., index goes from 0, to 1, 2, and back to 0).

- In the case where the player has two weapons (gun and automatic gun, gun and grenade, or grenade and automatic gun), we switch between the current and the second weapon.

- Finally if the player has only one weapon, nothing happens.
- We also print a message, in the **Console** window, that indicates the current weapon and the corresponding ammunitions.

Last but not least, you can modify the code in the **Start** method as follows.

```
hasWeapon [WEAPON_AUTO_GUN] = true;
```

Please save your code, and test the scene. As you press the *Tab* key, you should see the message "**Current Weapon: AUTOMATIC GUN (10)**" and "**Current Weapon: GUN (10)**" in the **Console** window.

Well, our system is working properly; now we just need to link it to the firing system, so that we can shoot depending on the current weapon and ammunitions available for this weapon.

Please modify the **Update** method as follows (new code in bold).

Creating and Managing Weapons

```
if (Input.GetKeyDown(KeyCode.F))
{
        if (currentWeapon == WEAPON_GUN && ammos [WEAPON_GUN] >=1 && canShoot)
        {
                ammos [currentWeapon]--;
                if (Physics.Raycast(rayFromPlayer, out hit, 100))
                {
                        print (" The object " + hit.collider.gameObject.name +" is in front of the player");
                        Vector3 positionOfImpact;
                        positionOfImpact = hit.point;
                        Instantiate     (sparksAtImpact,     positionOfImpact, Quaternion.identity);
                        GameObject objectTargeted;
                        if (hit.collider.gameObject.tag == "target")
                        {
                                print ("hit a target");
                                objectTargeted = hit.collider.gameObject;
        objectTargeted.GetComponent<ManageNPC>().gotHit();
                        }
                }
                canShoot = false;
                timer = 0.0f;
                timerStarted = true;
                //gunAmmo --;
        }
}
```

In the previous code:

- We check that the key F has been pressed.

- We then check whether the current weapon is a gun and that we have enough ammunitions left.

- If this is the case, we decrease the number of ammunitions and proceed as we did before.

- After we have managed to fire the gun, we set the variable **canShoot** to false; this is so that the gun can't be fired while it is reloading.

- We then set-up the timer that calculates how much time it will take for the gun to reload; when this timer is up, the player will be able to use the weapon again, provided that there are enough ammunitions. So here, the time (for the timer) is set to 0 and it will then start. These variables **timer** and **timerStarted** will be used in the code that we yet need to add in the script.

Before we can add this timer, we need to set the reload time for each weapon; please add the following code at the end of the the **Start** method, for the script **ManageWeapons**:

```
reloadTime [WEAPON_GUN] = 2.0f;
reloadTime [WEAPON_AUTO_GUN] = 0.5f;
reloadTime [WEAPON_GRENADE] = 3.0f;
```

In the previous code, we indicate that it will take 2 seconds for the gun to reload, .5 seconds for the automatic gun to reload, and 3 seconds to be able to throw another grenade.

- Please add the following code at the beginning of the **Update** method:

```
if (timerStarted)
{
    timer += Time.deltaTime;
    if (timer >= reloadTime [currentWeapon])
    {
        timerStarted = false;
        canShoot = true;
    }
}
```

- In this code, if the timer is started (this will happen just after a weapon has been used), we increase the time.

- Once the time reaches the reload time for the current weapon, we can then stop the timer, and make it possible for the player to shoot again.

So let's test this system; before we do so, let's modify the code slightly so that we have enough ammunition for the automatic gun. Please modify the following code in the **Update** method:

```
if (Input.GetKeyDown(KeyCode.F))
{
    if ((currentWeapon == WEAPON_GUN || currentWeapon == WEAPON_AUTO_GUN) && ammos [currentWeapon] >=1 && canShoot)
    {
```

In the previous code, we check whether the gun or the automatic gun are selected, that we have enough ammunitions and that the current weapon can be used (i.e., when the reload time has elapsed).

We can also modify the number of initial ammunitions for the automatic gun, by modifying the code in the **Start** method as follows (new code in bold):

[181]

Creating and Managing Weapons

```
ammos [WEAPON_GUN] = 10;
```
ammos [WEAPON_AUTO_GUN] = 10;
```
ammos [WEAPON_GRENADE] = 0;
```

To make sure that we hear when the gun is shot, and to tell the difference between the two guns, we will also add a sound when one of these is fired.

- Import the **gun_shot** sound for the resource pack into Unity.

- Select the object **FirstPersonCharacter** (which is within the object **FPSController**).

- Then add an **Audio Source** component to it by selecting: **Component | Audio | AudioSource** from the top menu.

- Once this is done, a new **Audio Source** component should be added to this object.

- You can look at its properties in the **Inspector** window.

- As you look at the **Inspector** window, in the section called **Audio Source**, please uncheck the option **Play on Awake** and drag and drop the **gun_shot** sound from the **Project** window to the variable called **Audio Clip**, as illustrated on the next figure.

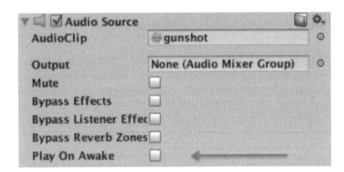

Figure 4-11: Adding an Audio Clip

Once this is done, we can trigger this sound through our script.

- Please open the script **ManageWeapons**.

- Modify the code in the **Update** method as follows (new code highlighted in bold).

```
if ((currentWeapon == WEAPON_GUN || currentWeapon == WEAPON_AUTO_GUN) && ammos [currentWeapon] >=1 && canShoot)
{
    ammos [currentWeapon]--;
```
GetComponent<AudioSource>().Play();

In the previous code, we access the **AudioSource** component on the object **FirstPersonCharacter**, and play the default **AudioClip** associated with this **Audio Source**.

The last change that we will make will be to display the current weapon onscreen.

- Please create a new **Text UI** object (**Game Object | UI | Text**).

- Rename this object **userInfo**.

- Please move this object to the bottom-left corner of the window (if it is not already there). You may switch to the 2D mode temporarily for this.

> To move the **Text UI** component you can temporarily switch to the 2D mode, this will display the screen boundaries (i.e., white rectangle) and make it easier to position the **Text UI** component. To activate or deactivate the 2D mode, you can click on the 2D icon located below the tab labeled scene, as described on the next figure.
>
>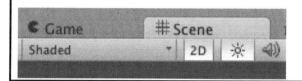

- You may change the color of the font for this text if you wish.

Next, we will modify the text for this object from the script to display the name of the current weapon:

- Please add the following code at the start of the script:

```
using UnityEngine.UI;
```

- The previous line makes it possible to refer to the **UI Text** component using the syntax **GetComponent<Text>**.

- Then add the following code at the end of the method **Update**.

```
GameObject.Find("userInfo").GetComponent<Text>().text = weaponName[currentWeapon]+ "("+ammos[currentWeapon]+")";
```

In the previous code, we access the **Text UI** object named **userInfo**, then its **Text** component; we then change the value of the text to the name of the current weapon.

We are now ready to go, so:

- Please save your code.

- Check for any error in the **Console** window.

- Play the scene.

- As you play the scene, try to switch between the two guns and see how the reload delay varies as you try to press the **F** key several times consecutively.

[183]

Creating and Managing Weapons

Now, at this stage, all works well; this being said we could just make a small change; that is, making it possible for the player to shoot repeatedly but without having to press the F key again; in other words, the weapon should fire, as long as the F key is kept pressed (or is down) and that we have sufficient ammos. For this, we just need to change the type of event detected. Instead of using the event **GetKeyDown**, we will use the event **GetKey**.

> While the first event (GetKeyDown) is triggered only when the key has been pressed, the second one (GetKey) is triggered as long as the key is being pressed.

Please modify the **Update** method in your code, for the conditional statement that checks whether the player has pressed the F key as follows:

```
if (Input.GetKey(KeyCode.F))
```

Play the scene and check that you can now fire consecutive shots by just keeping the F key pressed.

MANAGING THE COLLECTION OF AMMUNITIONS

Well, so far we have managed to define two different weapons and to fire them based on the corresponding ammunitions. What we need to do now is to make it possible, as we have done before, for the player to collect ammunitions, and to then update the game information accordingly. For this, we will need to do the following:

- Detect collision with ammo packs.

- Increase the number of ammunitions for a particular weapon.

- Destroy the ammo pack.

So let's modify the script **ManageWeapons** by editing the code for the method **manageCollisions** as follows.

```
public void manageCollisions (ControllerColliderHit hit)
{
      string tagOfTheOtherObject = hit.collider.gameObject.tag;
      if (tagOfTheOtherObject == "ammo_gun" || tagOfTheOtherObject ==
"ammo_automatic_gun" || tagOfTheOtherObject == "ammo_grenade")
      {
            int indexOfAmmoBeingUpdated = 0;
            if (tagOfTheOtherObject =="ammo_gun") indexOfAmmoBeingUpdated =
WEAPON_GUN;
            if (tagOfTheOtherObject =="ammo_automatic_gun")
indexOfAmmoBeingUpdated = WEAPON_AUTO_GUN;
            if (tagOfTheOtherObject =="ammo_grenade") indexOfAmmoBeingUpdated
= WEAPON_GRENADE;
            ammos [indexOfAmmoBeingUpdated] +=5;
            if (ammos [indexOfAmmoBeingUpdated] >
maxAmmos[indexOfAmmoBeingUpdated]) ammos[indexOfAmmoBeingUpdated] =
maxAmmos[indexOfAmmoBeingUpdated];
            Destroy (hit.collider.gameObject);
      }
}
```

In the previous code:

- We create a new string called **tagOfTheOtherObject**, to store the tag of the object that we are colliding with.

- We then check whether this object is an ammo pack (e.g., for a gun, an automatic gun or grenades).

Creating and Managing Weapons

- If this is the case, we check what type of ammos we have collided with and we keep track of its type using the variable **indexOfAmmoBeingUpdated**.

- Once this is done, we increase the number of ammos for the corresponding weapon (i.e., using the variable **indexOfAmmoBeingUpdated**).

- We then check that we have not reached the maximum number of ammos that we can carry for this particular weapon.

At this stage, you should have an ammo pack with a label called **ammo_gun** in your scene. So, with this in mind, please play the scene, collect this ammo pack and check that the number of ammos for your gun has increased.

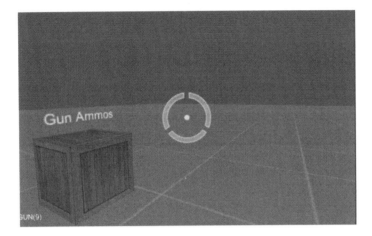

Figure 4-12: The gun ammos

We could now duplicate the object used for the ammunitions object, and change the duplicate's tag to **ammo_automatic_gun**.

- Please rename the object **Cube** (that is currently used for the ammunition) **ammo_gun**.

- Select this object.

- Duplicate this object (*CTRL + D*).

- Rename the duplicate **ammo_auto**.

- Create a new tag called **ammo_automatic_gun**.

- Apply the tag **ammo_automatic_gun** to the object **ammo_auto**.

- Using the **Scene** view, move the object **ammo_auto** apart from the other ammo pack.

- Play the scene and check that after collecting this pack (**ammo_auto**), your ammos for the automatic gun increase accordingly.

Once this is done, we will just add a 3D text to these boxes, so that it is easy to recognize them during gameplay.

- Please create a new 3D text object (**Game Object | 3D Object | 3D Text**).

- Rename this object **ammo_label**.

- Drag and drop this object on the object **ammo_gun**, so that it becomes a child of this object.

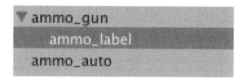

Figure 4-13: Setting the 3D text as a child of the ammo object

Then, select this object (**ammo_label**) and change its properties in the **Inspector** window as follows:

- Position: (**0, .8, 0**).

- Scale: (**0.15, 0.15, 0.15**).

- In the section called **Text Mesh**, change the **Text** attribute to **Gun Ammos**.

- In the section called **Text Mesh**, change the **Anchor** attribute to **Middle-centre**.

- In the section called **Text Mesh**, change the **Alignment** attribute to **Centre**.

- Once you have made these modifications, it should look as follows:

Creating and Managing Weapons

Figure 4-14: Adding 3D text to an object

- You can then repeat the previous steps to create a new 3D text label for the object **ammo_auto**, that displays the text "**Auto Gun Ammos**". You could, for example, duplicate the previous label, add the duplicate to the object **ammo_auto**, and change its position.

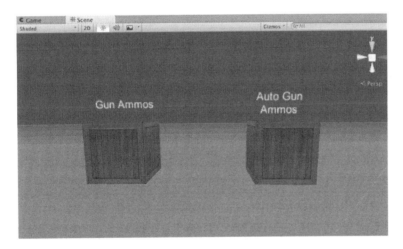

Figure 4-15: Two ammo packs with 3D labels

The last interesting detail we could add here, is to create prefabs from these packs, so that they can be instantiated or modified later.

Creating and Managing Weapons

- Drag and drop the object called **ammo_gun** to the **Project** window.
- This will create a prefab called **ammo_gun**.
- Repeat these steps for the object **ammo_auto**.

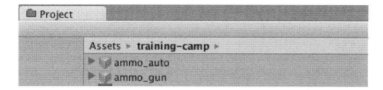

We can now:

- Deactivate the two ammos present in the scene.
- Drag and drop one of each of the ammo prefabs we have created (or more) to the scene. You may need to adjust their position so that they are above the ground, for example **y=1.2**.
- Play the scene to test whether we can still collect these ammos.

> By creating prefabs for these ammo packs, we have created templates that can be reused (or instantiated) either from the scene view (i.e., by dragging and dropping these prefabs to the scene), or from the code, by instantiating these prefabs while the game is playing. This is interesting, for example when you would like to balance the game difficulty and spawn some ammos when the player is in trouble and needs them.

CREATING A GRENADE LAUNCHER

At this stage our weapon management system works well; however, we just need to add the ability to throw grenades (and to also pick-up corresponding ammos). For this purpose, we will use rigid body physics, as we have in the last chapter, to propel the grenade and also apply damage, where applicable. For this purpose we will:

- Create a launcher attached to the player.

- When the **F** key is pressed and the grenade launcher is selected, we will propel a grenade in the direction where the player is looking, provided that we have enough ammunition.

- The grenade will explode after a few seconds.

- Upon explosion, all objects within a specific radius of the grenade will be destroyed.

So let's get started.

- Create a new empty object (**Game Object | Empty Object**) and rename it **launcher**.

- Drag and drop this object on top of the object **FirstPersonCharacter** (and NOT the **FPSCOntroller**), so that the launcher becomes a child of the object **FirstPersonCharacter**.

- Modify its position to **(0, 0, 0)**.

- Create a new **Sphere** object (**Game Object | 3D Object | Sphere**).

- Rename this object **grenade**.

- Modify its scale properties to **(0.2, 0.3, 0.2)**.

- You can also add a color to it if you wish.

- Add a **Rigidbody** component to this object (i.e., the grenade) by selecting: **Component | Physics | Rigidbody**.

Once this is done, we can start to modify our script **ManageWeapons** so that we can propel this grenade:

- Open the script **ManageWeapons**.

- Add the following code at the beginning of the class, to declare a placeholder that will be accessed from the **Inspector** to set the grenade that will be launched:

```
public GameObject grenade;
```

- Also modify the code in the **Start** method, to specify that we will start the game with a grenade launcher, as follows:

```
hasWeapon [WEAPON_GRENADE] = true;
```

- You can also add the following line within the **Start** method, so that we start with 10 grenades.

```
ammos [WEAPON_GRENADE] = 10;
```

Then we just need to add code to manage the grenades. The code that we are about to add will simply check whether we have a grenade, and the corresponding ammunitions for it. It will also instantiate and propel a grenade in the air.

- Please add the following code in the **Update** function, just after the code that deals with the guns (but within the conditional statements that deals with the key **F**; if ensure, you can always check the solution code included in the resource pack).

```
if (currentWeapon == WEAPON_GRENADE && ammos [WEAPON_GRENADE] >=1 && canShoot)
{
    ammos [currentWeapon]--;
    GameObject launcher = GameObject.Find("launcher");
    GameObject grenadeF = (GameObject) (Instantiate (grenade, launcher.transform.position, Quaternion.identity));
    grenadeF.GetComponent<Rigidbody>().AddForce(launcher.transform.forward*200);
    canShoot = false;
    timer = 0.0f;
    timerStarted = true;
}
```

In the previous code:

- We check if the grenade launcher is selected and that we have enough ammunition.
- We then decrease the corresponding level of ammunition.
- We identify the **launcher** object.
- We create a new instance of the object **grenade** (i.e., a public variable that will be set later by dragging and dropping the **grenade** object on it in the **Inspector**).
- The new projectile is then propelled using the method **AddForce**.

Once this is done, you can:

- Save your code.
- Create a new grenade prefab by dragging the **grenade** object to the **Project** window.

Creating and Managing Weapons

- Once this is done, we can deactivate the **grenade** object already present in the scene.

- We can also select the object **FirstPersonCharacter** and drag and drop the prefab **grenade** (from the **Project** window) to the field called **grenade** for the script **ManageWeapons** attached to the object **FirstPersonCharacter**. Once this is done, you can now test the scene, switch between weapons, and check that you can throw a grenade.

After this, we just need to create an explosion and also check if other objects are close to the grenade. For this purpose, we will create a new script that will be attached to the grenade that has been instantiated.

- Please create a new C# script called **Grenade**.

- Open the script and add the following code to it (new code in bold).

```csharp
public class Grenade : MonoBehaviour {
public float grenadeTimer;
public bool grenadeTimerStatrted;
public float grenadeTimerLimit;
public bool grenadeExplode;
public GameObject explosion;
private float radius = 5.0f;
private float power = 500.0f;
private float timer;
private float explosionTime;
private bool hasExploded;
```

In the previous script, we declare several variables that will be necessary to control and launch the grenade: variables that will determine when the grenade should explode (e.g., **grenadeTimer**, **grenadeTimerStarted**, and **grenadeTimerLimit**), a variable that checks whether the grenade has exploded (**grenadeExplode**), the radius within which objects will be affected by the explosion, and the power of the explosion.

- Then we can modify the method **Start** as follows:

```csharp
private void Start ()
{
    timer = 0.0f; explosionTime = 2.0f;
    hasExploded = false;
}
```

In the previous code:

- We set the explosion time to 2 seconds, so that the grenade explodes two seconds after it has been propelled.

- We also specify that it has not exploded yet.

- Finally, we will modify the method **Update** as follows:

```
void Update()
{
    timer+=Time.deltaTime;
    if (timer >= explosionTime)
    {
        if (hasExploded == false)
        {
            Vector3 explosionPos = gameObject.transform.position;
            Collider [] colliders = Physics.OverlapSphere (explosionPos, radius);
            for (int i = 0; i < colliders.Length; i++)
            {
                if (colliders [i].gameObject.GetComponent<Rigidbody>() != null && colliders [i].gameObject.tag != "Player")
                {
                    GameObject objectTargeted = colliders [i].gameObject;
                    if (objectTargeted.tag == "target") objectTargeted.GetComponent<ManageNPC>().gotHitByGrenade();
                }
            }
            hasExploded = true;
            Destroy (gameObject);
        }
    }
}
```

In the previous code:

- We update the time.

- We also check whether the grenade should detonate (based on **explosionTime**).

- In this case, we look for all objects around the grenade with a **Rigidbody** component (i.e., these objects should be affected by the force exerted by the grenade); for this purpose we use the method **Physics.OverlapSphere**.

> The method **Physics.OverlapSphere** checks for the presence of rigid bodies within a specific radius; in our case, once they have been found, the colliders of these objects are saved in the variable called **colliders**.

As you can see in the previous code, we are referring to a method called **goHitByGrenade**, from the script **ManageNPC**; however, this method does not exist yet, and you may have an error in the **Console** window for this reason.

Creating and Managing Weapons

So let's modify the script **ManageNPC** accordingly:

- Please open the script **ManageNPC**.
- Add the following code to it:

```
public void gotHitByGrenade()
{
     print ("Hit by grenade");
     health = 0;
}
```

In the previous code, we set the health of the NPC to 0 if it has been hot by a grenade.

Now that the code is compiled correctly, we can update the prefab grenade:

- Please drag and drop the script **Grenade** on the object **grenade** in the **Scene** view (this object is deactivated at present).
- Select this object (i.e., grenade).
- Activate this object.
- Using the **Inspector** window, check that the script **Grenade** is now a component of the object **grenade**.
- Using the **Inspector** window, click on the button **Apply** located in the top-right corner of the **Inspector** window to be able to update the corresponding prefab.

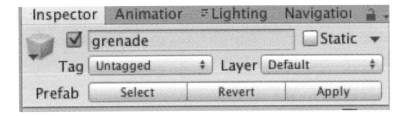

Figure 4-16: Updating the grenade prefab

- You can now deactivate this object again. It is important to apply the changes to an activated object; otherwise, if changes were applied while the object is deactivated, the object within the prefab would, in turn, also be deactivated.

> To update a prefab, you can either update the object that was used to create the prefab, and then **Apply** the changes to the prefab, or select the prefab and amend it directly.

Before we can test the scene, we just need to make sure that all the targets include a rigid body, so that the explosion affects them:

[194]

Creating and Managing Weapons

- Please select all the targets in the scene.

- Add a rigid body component to these targets using **Component | Physics | Rigidbody**.

- You can now save your code, and test the scene. As you test the scene, switch to your grenade launcher and throw some grenades. You should see that the targets within range disappear with smoke left at their previous location.

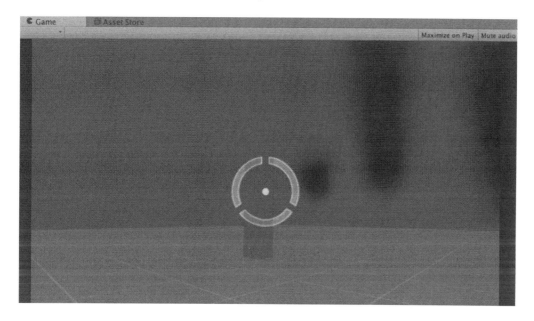

Figure 4-17: The targets disappear after being hit several times.

So, the grenades work quite well; however, it would be great to add a more visual effect, for example, using an explosion at the point of impact. For this purpose, we will instantiate an explosion (just as we have done in the previous chapter), where the grenade has exploded.

- Please select the prefab **grenade** in the **Project** window.

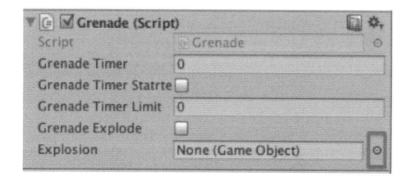

Figure 4-18: Adding an explosion to the grenade

[195]

- Using the **Inspector**, click on the circle to the right of the variable **explosion** to select a prefab for this explosion, as illustrated on the previous figure.

- In the next window, search for the word **explosion**, and choose the **explosion** prefab from the results returned.

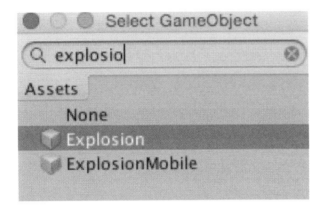

Figure 4-19: Selecting a new explosion for the grenade

Once this is done, we just need to change the code in the script called **Grenade** to instantiate a new explosion when it detonates.

- Please open the script **Grenade** and add the following code in the **Update** method (new code in bold).

GameObject.Instantiate (explosion, transform.position, Quaternion.identity);
```
hasExploded = true;
Destroy (gameObject);
```

- In the previous code we instantiate a new explosion at the point where the grenade has detonated.

- Please save your code and test the scene.

As you try to launch a grenade, it will explode; however, some of the targets that are not within range may be propelled in the air.

So, what we could do, is to give a very high weight to the targets, so that they are not propelled in the air by the explosion:

- Please select all the targets available in the scene.

- Using the **Inspector**, change their mass from 1 to 10000 (using the **Rigidbody** component).

- Play the scene again, and you should see that the targets that are not within range are not blown away by the explosion.

Last but not least, we need to create ammos for the grenades.

- Using the **Project** window, duplicate the **ammo_gun** prefab.

- Rename it **ammo_grenade**.

- Select this new prefab (i.e., **ammo_grenade**).

- Create a new tag **ammo_grenade**, and apply it to this prefab.

- Drag and drop this new prefab (i.e., **ammo_grenade**) to the scene, and adjust its position, if need be, so that it is above the ground.

- As you add it to the scene, it will create a new instance of the prefab in the scene named **ammo_grenade**; within this object, there should also be a **GUI Text** object named **ammo_label**, as described on the next figure.

Figure 4-20: Selecting the label for the grenade ammos

- Please select this object, and modify the text for its label to **Grenade Ammos**, as described on the next figure.

Figure 4-21: Modifying the text for the label of the grenade ammos

Once this is done, we can update the **grenade_ammo** prefab so that all objects instantiated from this prefab have the correct label, by clicking on the button **Apply** located in the top-right corner of the **Inspector** window, or by dragging and dropping the object **ammo_grenade** on the prefab **ammo_grenade**. This is another simple way to update the prefab.

Once this is done, you can test the scene. You may notice that the initial number of grenades is 10 and that it then drops to 5 after collecting the grenade ammos; this is because we have initialized the number of grenades to 10 in our code and set the maximum to 5; so we could change our code in the **Start** method for the script **ManageWeapons** as follows:

```
maxAmmos [WEAPON_GRENADE] = 10;
```

You can also create a new prefab for the First-Person Controller by dragging and dropping the object **FPSController** to the **Project** window, so that we can reuse it in other levels, at a later stage. You can use any name of your choice, for example, **player_with_launcher**.

LEVEL ROUNDUP

In this chapter, we have further improved our skills to learn about how to create a complete weapon management system. We became more comfortable with rays, arrays, and particles. We managed to create scripts to detect objects in the distance, fire a weapon, propel a projectile in the air, or instantiate explosions. We also optimized our game and code by creating prefabs, methods, constant variables, and arrays. So, again, we have made considerable progress since the last chapter. Well done!

Checklist

You can consider moving to the next stage if you can do the following:

- Create a **ray**.
- Create and instantiate prefabs.
- Detect objects ahead with a ray.
- Detect key strokes.
- Instantiate explosions.
- Manage and account for ammunitions.

Quiz

It's time to check your knowledge. Please answer the following questions.

1. A new prefab can be created by dragging and dropping an object to the **Project** window.

2. The following code will empty the text for the component named **userMessageUI**.

```
GameObject.Find("userMessageUI").GetComponent.<UI.Text>.text ="";
```

3. To be able to instantiate a prefab, the following code could be used:

```
Instantiate (prefab, transform.position, Quaternion.identity);
```

4. Find one error in the following code.

```
void OnControllerColliderHit (ControllerColliderHit hit)
{
    if (hit.collider.tag = "pick_me") print ("Collided with a box");
}
```

5. Any prefab can be duplicated using the shortcut *CTRL + F*.

6. If the object **myObject** does not have a Rigidbody component, and the following code is used, an error message will be displayed in the **Console** window.

```
myObject.GetComponent<Rigidbody>().AddForce (transform.forward*100);
```

7. What does this error message most likely mean "**; missing**".

   a) You have forgotten to declare a variable.
   b) One of the statements in your code is missing a semi-colon.
   c) The method that you have called does not exist.

8. There is only one way to add an **Audio Source** component to an object, and this is using the button **Add Component** button in the **Inspector** window for this object.

9. If the method **manageCollision** is defined as follows...

```
public void manageCollision()
{
    print ("Collision detected");
}
```

... it can be called from outside its containing class.

10. The following code will create an array and then access its first element.

```
int [] myArray = new int [4];
int newVar = myArray [1];
```

Solutions to the Quiz

1. TRUE.

2. TRUE.

3. TRUE.

4.
```
void OnControllerColliderHit (ControllerColliderHit hit)
{
    if (hit.collider.gameObject.tag = "pick_me") print ("Collided with a box");
}
```

5. FALSE.

6. TRUE.

7. c (missing semi-colon)

8. FALSE.

9. TRUE.

10. FALSE (the second element is accessed in the code).

Challenge 1

Now that you have managed to complete this chapter and that you have improved your skills, let's put these to the test.

- Add more ammos to the scene, based on the prefabs that you have created earlier (i.e., drag and drop the prefabs to the scene).
- Test the scene and check that you can collect them and increase your ammunitions.

Challenge 2

- Create a new **UI Text** object
- Update the text for this object with the message "**You have just collected ammos**" every time you pick up an ammo pack.
- Using one of the sounds located in the resource pack, play a sound whenever an ammo pack has been collected.

5
USING FINITE STATE MACHINES

In this section, we start to work with Finite State Machines (FSM) to be able to manage NPCs and how they behave depending on the environment. We will also get to design some basic, intermediate and advanced artificial intelligence along with animated characters.

After completing this chapter, you will be able to:

- Create and manage a Finite State Machine.
- Associate character animations to different states.
- Use the FSM to implement basic and intermediate types of artificial intelligence.
- Simulate vision detection for the NPCs.
- Get the NPCs to behave realistically.

INTRODUCTION TO FINITE STATE MACHINES

So, you have probably heard about state machines in the past, but may not know exactly what it means. In a nutshell, when you create a game, you will most probably use Non-Player Characters (NPCs). These characters will probably have some levels of artificial intelligence.

When applying these different levels of intelligence, we usually want to mimic how people would behave in real life. This means that based on specific factors (e.g., low ammos or enemy in sight), the NPC will follow a specific behavior.

This behavior is often broken down into states. That is, we consider that at any time during the game, the NPC is in only one state. So the NPC will be either idle, following the player, shooting at the player, or looking for health packs.

Now, when we consider states, we also need to consider how (and why) the NPC will enter or exit a state. For example, at the start of the game, our NPC could be idle (state = **IDLE**), and then, if the NPC sees the player, it will transition to the **Follow Player** state. While following the player, the NPC may lose sight of the player, and then decide to go back to its initial position (state = **Go Back To Initial Position**), and once it has reached its initial position, it will be **IDLE** again.

So what we can see here, is that we have different states, and there are triggers and/or conditions to enter or exit a state.

Now, this is of course just one possible behavior, and we could create several different behaviors to implement different types of NPCs; but in all cases, this behavior will be determined by states, transitions, and conditions that will need to be fulfilled to transition between states.

In Unity, you can define states and transition very easily using a visual tool that makes it possible to define states, to define variables that will be assessed for transitions, and to define and check for conditions that need to be fulfilled so that transitions between states can occur. These tools are available in the **Animator** window, and we will learn to use these in the next section.

GETTING STARTED WITH FINITE-STATE MACHINES IN UNITY

In this section, we will become familiar with creating a simple FSM and applying it to an NPC.

- Please save your current scene.

- Create a new scene (**File | New Scene**).

- Create a new **Animator Controller** by selecting **Create | Animator Controller** from the **Project** window.

- Rename this controller **guard**. This should create an **Animator Controller**. An **Animator Controller** is effectively a way to create and manage different states. This animator controller will then be attached to an NPC to control its behavior.

> **Animator Controllers** are used to define states and also rules for transitioning between these states. They control how an object (e.g., NPC) may behave under certain conditions.

- Please display the **Animator** window by selecting: **Window | Animator**. You may change the layout of Unity as illustrated in the next figure.

- The following window will appear.

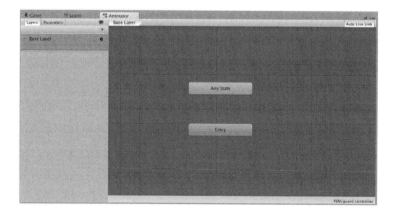

Figure 5-1: Creating a new Animator Controller

You will see that, by default, the **Animator Controller** will have two states symbolized by rectangles: a state called **Any State** and an **Entry** State. The first state (i.e., **Any State**) will be covered later in this book, and it used to define general behaviors that apply to any state (hence the name **Any State**). The **Entry** state is the point of entry for our behavior. In other words, when the FSM is started, it will be in that state. So what we will do now is to create a new state called **IDLE** in which our player will be at the start of the game (so the FSM will transition to this state at the start of the game).

Using Finite State Machines

- Please right-click on the grid (or canvas) in the **Animator** window, and select **Create State | Empty** from the contextual menu. This will create a new state called **New State** symbolized by an orange rectangle.

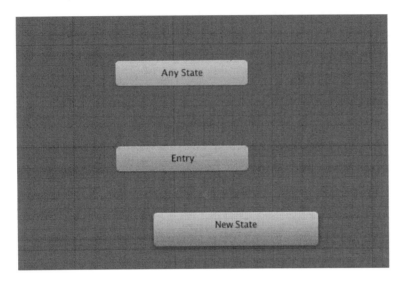

Figure 5-2: Creating a new state

- You may notice an arrow from the state **Entry** to the state **New State**. So by default, when we start the game, the new state **New Sate** will be entered.

- Let's rename this new state: select this state (i.e., **New State**) by clicking once on it, and change its name to **IDLE**, using the **Inspector** window.

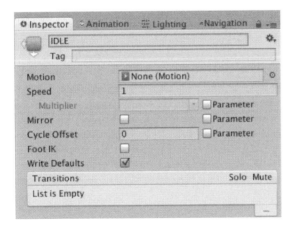

Figure 5-3: Changing the name of the state

- As you make this change, you may look at the other fields in the **Inspector** window, you will notice fields called **motion** (this will be used later in this book to add an animation), **speed** (the speed of the animation), or **transitions**.

[206]

Using Finite State Machines

- Once this is done, we can create a new state called **FOLLOW_PLAYER**, using the same method as previously (*CTRL + Click*, and then select **Create State | Empty**).

- Once this is done, we will create a transition between the states **IDLE** and **FOLLOW_PLAYER**, so that the FSM transitions to the later based on a condition; however, before we can specify the transition, we need to define variables. This is because the conditions used for the transitions are based on variables that we need to declare. As we will see, these variables can be of different types including **Boolean**, **string**, or **integer**. So let's create one of these parameters.

- Within the **Animator** window, click on the tab called **Parameters**.

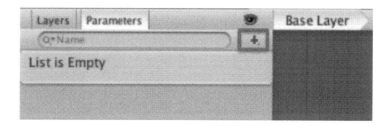

Figure 5-4: Adding a parameter (part 1)

- At present the list is empty, as we haven't defined any parameter yet.

- Please click on the + button, as highlighted on the previous figure, and select **Bool** from the contextual menu, so that you can create a **Boolean** variable.

Figure 5-5: Adding a parameter (part 2)

- This should create a new **Boolean** parameter. The box to its left is unchecked, which means that its value is **false** by default. Please rename this variable **canSeePlayer** (e.g., you can double-click on the default name and then change it).

Once this is done, we can create a transition between the states **IDLE** and **FOLLOW_PLAYER**.

- Please right-click on the state **IDLE**, select **Make Transition** from the contextual menu, and click on the state **FOLLOW_PLAYER**. This should create a transition between these two states, symbolized by an arrow.

Using Finite State Machines

> If need be, you can always delete a transition by right-clicking on it and then select the option to **Delete**.

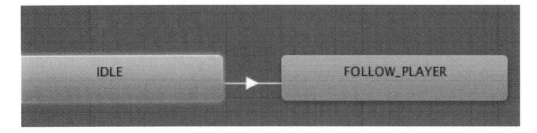

Figure 5-6: Creating a transition

Once this is done, we just need to specify when this transition should occur:

- Please select the transition by clicking on it once (i.e., the white arrow between the two states).

- This should display information about this transition in the **Inspector** window.

Figure 5-7: Displaying information about the transition

- You may also notice a section called **Conditions** at the bottom of the **Inspector** window, and we will use it to specify when the transition will occur (or what conditions should be fulfilled for this transition to occur).

- Please click on the + sign, as illustrated on the next figure.

Using Finite State Machines

Figure 5-8: Setting the condition for the transition (part 1)

Because we only have one parameter declared (i.e., **canSeePlayer**), Unity will automatically set the transition condition to **canSeePlayer = true**.

Figure 5-9: Setting the condition for the transition

- This means that the transition will occur only if this parameter is equal to true.

So at this stage, we have defined states and a basic rule that defines when the FSM should transition from the **IDLE** to the **FOLLOW_PLAYER** state. So, we now need to apply this FSM to an object and see how it works. For this purpose, we will create a simple object and attach the FSM to it. Note that nothing really happens in these states right now, but in the next section we will see how we can define what the NPC does in these states and what animations can be used for this purpose (e.g., idle, walking, etc.).

- Please create an empty object (**GameObject | Create Empty**) and rename it **testFSM**.

- Drag and drop the **Animator Controller** called **guard** that we have just created earlier, from the **Project** window to the object **testFSM** (e.g., using the **Inspector** or the **Scene** view). This will create a new component called **Animator** for the object **testFSM**. You will notice, as illustrated on the next figure, that this animator has several parameters, including a parameter called **Controller**. This controller is, in our case, the **Animator Controller** that we have created (i.e., guard). In other words, the object **testFSM** may be animated (or have a specific behavior) and this behavior will be **controlled** by the **Animator Controller** called **guard**.

Using Finite State Machines

Figure 5-10: Adding an Animator component

It is now time to test our **Animator Controller**.

- Please select the object **testFSM**.
- Play the scene.
- Click on the tab **Animator**, so that you can see the **Animator Controller**.
- You should see a blue line under the state **IDLE**; it means that this is the active state.

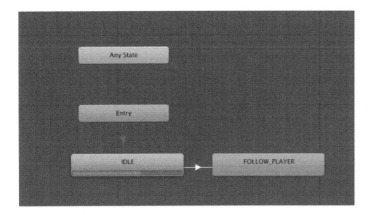

Figure 5-11: Observing our Animator Controller

> Note that you can pan the view within the **Animator** window by pressing the **ALT** key and dragging and dropping your mouse.

- Now, let's try to see if the transition is working: in the **parameter** tab within the **Animator** window, check the box for the parameter **canSeePlayer**. This will set this variable to true, and the transition to the next state (**FOLLOW_PLAYER**) should occur, as illustrated on the next figure.

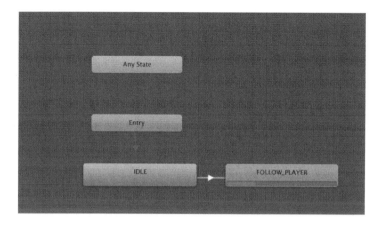

Figure 5-12: Transitioning from IDLE to FOLLOW_PLAYER

Eh Voila!

You can now stop playing the scene.

Now, you may be wondering, "Ok, this is great, but how can I link this behavior to an NPC or an object in the scene".

Well, so far we have been able to test the FSM from the **Animator** window, but there is, of course, a way to control this animator (and trigger transitions) through scripting, and we will discover how this can be done in the next section.

CONTROLLING AN ANIMATOR CONTROLLER FROM A C# SCRIPT

So at this stage, you might be comfortable with the idea of states, transitions, and **Animator Controller**; what we will do here is to control the **Animator Controller**, that we have created earlier, from our script; so we will be able to:

- Access this **Animator Controller**.
- Check what state we are in (i.e., the active state).
- Perform actions depending on the active state.
- Set values for parameters so that transitions can occur between states.

So let's get started:

- Create a new C# script called **ControlNPCFSM**.

- Drag and drop this script on the object **testFSM**.

- Once this is done, we can open our script and start editing it, bearing in mind that, because it is attached to the object **testFSM**, we will be able to access its components directly, including the **Animator Controller**.

- Please modify the code as follows (new code in bold).

```
using UnityEngine;
using System.Collections;

public class ControlNPCFSM : MonoBehaviour
{
    private Animator anim;
    // Use this for initialization
    void Start ()
    {
        anim = GetComponent<Animator>();
    }
    // Update is called once per frame
    void Update ()
    {
        if (Input.GetKeyDown (KeyCode.I))
        {
            anim.SetBool("canSeePlayer", true);
        }
    }
}
```

In the previous code:

- We declare a new variable of type Animator, called **anim**.

- This variable is initialized in the **Start** method, so that it points to the **Animator** component of the object **testFSM**.

- We then, using the **Update** function, detect whether the key **I** has been pressed; if this is the case, we set the value of the parameter **canSeePlayer** to true. For this purpose we use the method **anim.SetBool**; for this method, we pass two parameters: the name of the parameter to be altered (using quotes), and its new value.

> It is possible to set the values of parameters defined in a particular **Animator Controller** from a script using the methods **SetBool**, **SetString**, or **SetInt**.

Once this is done, we can save our script and test it:

- Please play the scene.

- You may move the **Game** window beside the **Console** window, so that you can see both the **Game** and the **Animator** window simultaneously. This will be helpful because we will need to click on the **Game** window before pressing the I key, so that the **Game** window is active, and so that pressing the **I** key can be detected (and processed).

- Click once on the **Game** view.

Using Finite State Machines

- Press the **I** key.

- Look at the **Animator** window and check that the **Animator Controller** has transitioned to the **FOLLOW_PLAYER** state.

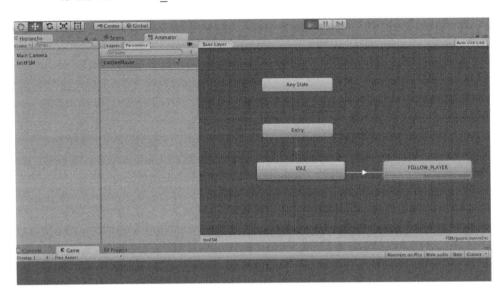

Figure 5-13: Triggering the transition from a script

Once you have checked that this is working, we will add another transition to this **Animator Controller**, so that the NPC goes back to the **IDLE** state when he can't see the player anymore.

> Whenever you make a modification to your game, please ensure that it is not playing, as any change made as the game is playing will not be kept.

- You can stop playing the scene.

- Please select the object **testFSM**.

- Open the **Animator** window.

- Create a new transition from the state **FOLOW_PLAYER** to the state **IDLE** (i.e., right-click on the **FOLLOW_PLAYER** state and select **Make Transition**).

Using Finite State Machines

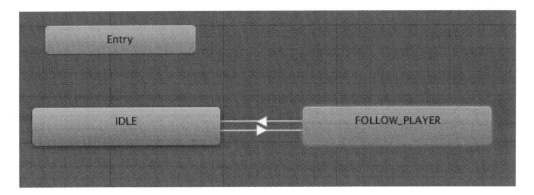

Figure 5-14: Creating a new transition to the IDLE state

- We can then select the transition and apply the condition **canSeePlayer = false** for this transition to occur (using the **Inspector**).

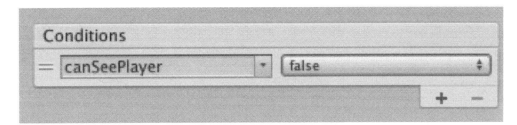

Figure 5-15: Setting the condition for the transition

> Note that transitions can be based on a combination of conditions (i.e., by checking the value of several parameters).

- We can now modify our C# script (**ControlNPCFSM**) as follows (new code in bold).

[215]

Using Finite State Machines

```
void Update ()
{
        if (Input.GetKeyDown (KeyCode.I))
        {
                anim.SetBool("canSeePlayer", true);
        }
        if (Input.GetKeyDown (KeyCode.J))
        {
                anim.SetBool("canSeePlayer", false);
        }
}
```

In the previous code, we check whether the key **J** was pressed. If this is the case, we then change the value of the parameter **canSeePlayer** to **false**, so that the transition back to the state **IDLE** can occur.

Please save your code, and play the scene. Click once in the **Game** window (so that this window is active and that the key strokes are detected). As you successively press the **I** and **J** keys, you should see that the **Animator Controller** transitions to the state **FOLLOW_PLAYER**, and then back to the state **IDLE**.

LINKING TRANSITIONS TO THE MOVEMENT OF OBJECTS

At this stage, I assume that you find it easy to understand how to control parameters from a script. However, what we could do now is to literally control the movement of an object based on the **Animator Controller**. So, we will use the controller that we have already created, and modify the associated script so that:

- The NPC will be, for the time being, symbolized by a cube.

- The NPC will be idle at the start of the scene.

- A ray is created (or casted) from the NPC and pointing forward.

- If this ray detects the player, then the NPC will start to look in the direction of the player and then move in its direction.

- Whenever the NPC loses sight of the player, it will stop on its track.

So this is a very simple behavior, to start with, and we will then customize it to add more states. So let's get started!

- Please create a ground for the scene: create a new box, at the position **(0,0,0)**, scaled on the x- and z-axis by **100** and with a texture of your choice.

- Modify the ambient light for this scene so that it is a light color (**Window | Lighting**).

- Create a new **Cube**, apply a color to it (e.g., green), rename it **NPC**, and place it just above the ground.

- Add an **FPSController** prefab to the scene from the folder **Standard Assets | Characters | FirstPersonCharacter | Prefab**.

- Assign the tag **Player** to this object.

- Deactivate the object **Main Camera** as well as the object **testFSM**.

- Select the **NPC** object, add an **Animator** component to it (**Component | Miscellaneous | Animator**), and drag and drop the **guard Animation Controller** from the **Project** window to the field called **Controller** for the **Animator** component of the object **NPC**, as described on the next figure.

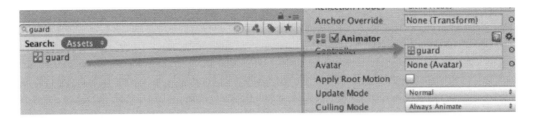

Figure 5-16: Adding the Animator Controller called guard (part 1)

Figure 5-17: Adding the Animator Controller called guard (part 2)

- Add the script **ControlNPCFSM** to the object **NPC** (i.e., drag and drop this script on the object NPC).

So our NPC is now linked to the **Animator Controller**; it includes an **Animator** component, that is controlled by the **guard Animator Controller**, and its also includes the script **ControlNPCFSM** that we will use to access the **Animator Controller**.

We will now modify this script to create the ray casting and also change the **Animator Controller**'s parameters based on whether the player is in sight.

- Please open the script **ControlNPCFSM**.

- Add the following code at the start of the class (new code in bold).

```
public class ControlNPCFSM : MonoBehaviour {
private Animator anim;
private Ray ray;
private RaycastHit hit;
private AnimatorStateInfo info;
private string objectInSight;
```

In the previous code, we declare five variables:

- The variable **anim** will be used to link-up to the **Animator Controller** component of the object **NPC**.

- The variable **ray** will be used to cast a ray and detect objects ahead.

- The variable **hit** will be used to collect information about the collision between the ray casted and objects ahead.

- The variable **info** will be used to determine the current state for our **Animator Controller**.

- The variable **objectInSight** is used to store the tag of the object currently in sight (if any).

Next, let's modify the **Update** method by adding the following code to it (at the end of the method).

```
ray.origin = transform.position;
ray.direction = transform.forward;
info = anim.GetCurrentAnimatorStateInfo(0);
objectInSight = "";
```

In the previous code:

- We set the origin of the ray. In this case it will originate from the position of the NPC (i.e., linked to this script).

- We then set the direction of the ray (i.e., forward).

- We then initialize the variable **info**. By accessing the current state of the **Animator Controller** using the method **GetCurrentAnimatorStateInfo(0)**. Note that the parameter **0** refers to the first layer of the **Animator Controller**.

Using Finite State Machines

> There can be several layers for a particular **Animator Controller**, and in our case, only one (i.e., the first one) has been used. The number of layers can be checked using the **Animator** window, through the **Layer** tab, as illustrated on the next figure.

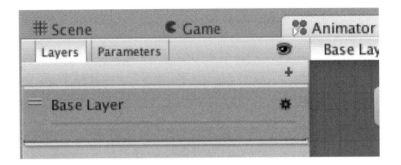

Figure 5-18: Checking the number of layers

- In the previous figure, there is only one layer for this **Animator Controller**, and it is called **Base Layer**.

Please add the following code, just after the code we have added in the **Update** method:

```
Debug.DrawRay (ray.origin, ray.direction * 100, Color.red);
if (Physics.Raycast(ray.origin, ray.direction * 100, out hit))
{
     objectInSight = hit.collider.gameObject.tag;
     print ("Object in Sight" + objectInSight);
     if (objectInSight == "Player")
     {
          anim.SetBool ("canSeePlayer",true);
          print ("Just saw the Player");
     }
}
```

In the previous code:

- We use the ray defined earlier, and cast it for debugging purposes (i.e., only seen in the **Scene** view), using the method **Debug.DrawLine**. Again, this is just for debugging purposes to visually check that the ray is pointing in the right direction.

- After this, we cast a ray using the syntax **Physics.Raycast**; this casts a ray from the NPC and forward.

- If the ray hits a collider, we save the tag of the object in front of the NPC and also print it.

- We then check for the name of the object in sight (if any).

Using Finite State Machines

- If this is the player, then we change the parameter **canSeePlayer** to true and also print a message in the **Console** window.

Please add the following code after the last code (i.e., at the end of the method **Update**).

```
if (info.IsName("IDLE"))
{
    print("We are in the IDLE state");
}
```

In the previous code:

- Using the variable **info**, which points to the state of the **Animator Controller**, we check if the current state is **IDLE**; if this is the case, we just print the text **"We are in the IDLE state"**.

We are almost there, we just need to include the following code after the code that you have just added:

```
else if (info.IsName("FOLLOW_PLAYER"))
{
    transform.LookAt(GameObject.Find("FPSController").transform);
    if (objectInSight != "Player")
    {
        anim.SetBool ("canSeePlayer",false);
        print ("Just lost sight of the Player");
    }
    else
    {
        transform.Translate(Vector3.forward* Time.deltaTime);
    }
    print("We are in the FOLLOW_PLAYER state");
}
```

In the previous code:

- We follow the same method used in the previous **if** statement by testing if the player is in sight.

- We look in the direction of the player using the method **LookAt**.

- If the player is not in sight then the parameter **canSeePlayer** is set to **false**.

- Otherwise, the NPC will start to move towards the player at the speed of **1** meter per second.

Using Finite State Machines

You can comment or delete the code that detects whether the player has pressed the keys **I** or **J**, as we will trigger events based on sight for now.

One of the last things we need to do is to add a wall to the scene, so that we can create a situation whereby the NPC loses sight of the player as it is following the player.

- Please create a cube, and add it to the scene, making sure that it is slightly above the ground, high enough (e.g., y scale of 4), and wide enough (e.g., x scale of 14).

- You can also create a new material (e.g., blue) and apply it to the wall.

Once this is done, we can now save our code and play the scene to check that:

- The NPC follows the player and transitions from the **IDLE** state to the **FOLLOW_PLAYER** state, once it "sees" the player.

- The NPC stops after losing sight of the player.

Once this is done we will, instead of using a box to represent our NPC, use an actual animated character.

USING ANIMATED CHARACTERS WITH MECANIM

In this section, we will replace our cubic NPC with an animated character and make some modifications to our script also.

First, let's import the animated character:

- In Unity, create a new folder (if you wish, so that it easier to find your animations) in the **Project** window (for example **military**).

- In your file system, please locate the folder called **animations** in the resource pack. Then locate the folder called **military** within the folder **animations**.

- Drag and drop the content of this folder (i.e., all files within the folder **military**) into your **Project** window (e.g., to the new folder that you have just created).

- Unity will then import these assets.

- If a window labeled **NormalMap Settings** appears, you can press the option to **Fix Now**, as illustrated on the next figure.

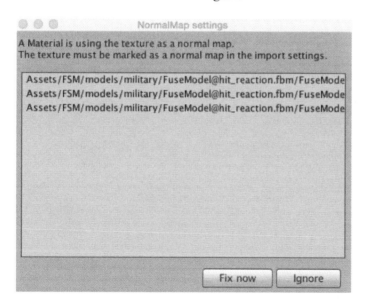

Figure 5-19: Fixing normals for imported models

- This should add several prefabs and folders that we will be able to use for the character animation.

Using Finite State Machines

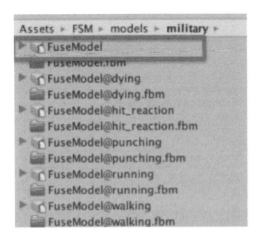

Figure 5-20: Completing the import

- Please deactivate the object called **NPC** already present in the scene.
- Drag the prefab **FuseModel** (as illustrated in the previous figure) to the **Scene** view.

Figure 5-21: Importing the model without animations

- You will notice that, for now, it is in what is called a **T pose**. However, this will change once we add animations for the different states.
- Rename this object **NPC1**.
- Attach the script **ControlNPCFSM** to it.
- Drag and drop the **Animator Controller** called **guard** from the **Project** window to this object (i.e., **NPC1**).

[224]

Using Finite State Machines

- By dragging and dropping the two previous assets to the object **NPC1**, we make sure that we can control the different states associated with our new NPC.

It is now time to configure the different states so that the object is animated depending on its state:

- Please select the object **NPC1**.

- Open the **Animator** window.

- Click on the state called **IDLE**.

- In the **Inspector** window, you will notice that the attribute **Motion** is empty.

- Please click on the circle to the right of the label **None (Motion)**, as illustrated on the next figure.

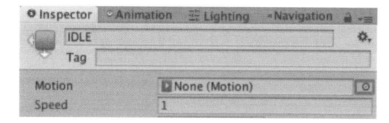

Figure 5-22: Setting the animation for the IDLE state

- In the new window, search for the animation **idle** and select it (e.g., type the text **idle** in the search field and then click on the animation **idle**).

Once this is done, we can perform a quick check by playing the scene. Since the **NPC** is in the **IDLE** mode, you will see it in an **IDLE** posture; however, it seems static (immobile); this is because we need to specify that its animation should loop.

Using Finite State Machines

Figure 5-23: The NPC in IDLE mode

So let's modify this clip to add a looping feature:

- Please stop playing the scene.

- Open the **Project** window and/or rearrange the layout of Unity so that you can see both the **Project** and the **Animation** window simultaneously.

- After making sure that the object **NPC1** is selected, use the **Animator** window to double-click on the clip **idle** that you have now added to the **IDLE** state.

- Its location should now be highlighted in yellow in the **Project** window.

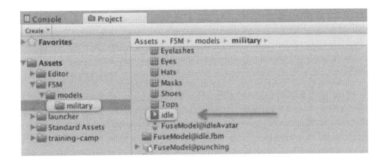

Figure 5-24: Finding the idle animation clip

- Once this is done, click on the animation clip **idle** (i.e., the one highlighted in yellow in the previous figure, in the **Project** view), this will display its properties.

- Using the **Inspector** window, click on the button **Edit** located in its top-right corner.

[226]

Using Finite State Machines

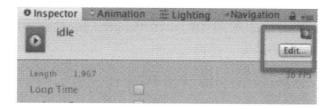

Figure 5-25: Editing an animation clip

- Once this is done, you can scroll down within the **Inspector** window, check (i.e., click on) the box **LoopTime**, so that the animation can loop indefinitely, and then press the button labeled **Apply** that is located in the bottom-right corner of the **Inspector** window, so that your changes can be applied and saved.

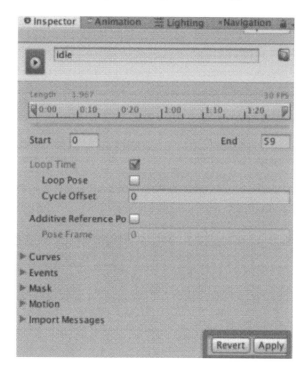

Figure 5-26: Adjusting the parameters of the animation clip

- After applying this change, you can play the scene, zoom-in on the object **NPC1** and check that it is animated and that the animation is looping.

> Whenever you apply modifications to your scene, please stop playing the scene, so that these modifications can be saved.

Next, we need to add an animation for the **FOLLOW_PLAYER** state:

- Select the object **NPC1**.

[227]

Using Finite State Machines

- Display the **Animator** window.

- In the **Animator** window, click on the state **FOLLOW_PLAYER**.

- Using the search field that is within the **Project** window, look for all animations in the **Project** by typing **t:animation**.

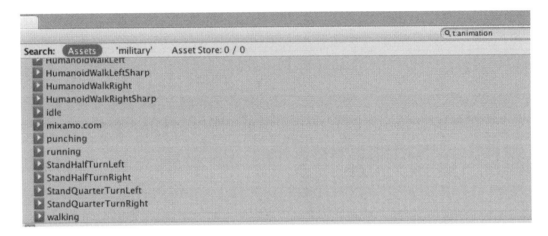

Figure 5-27: Searching for all the animations included in the project

- You can then drag and drop the animation **walking** from the results to the empty field for the attribute **Motion** of the state **FOLLOW_PLAYER**. This is another simple way of selecting an animation for a particular state.

Last but not list, we will add a mechanism that makes the ray casting from the NPC a bit more efficient; this will consist in creating an empty object, adding this object as a child of the **FPSController**, and using it as a target for the **NPC** when it casts rays to detect and follow the player.

- Please create an empty object and rename it **playerMiddle**.

- Add this object as a child of the object **FPSController**.

- Change its position to **(0, -0.67, 0)**.

Once this is done, we just need to modify our script:

- Please open the script **ControlNPCFSM**.

- Replace the line...

```
transform.LookAt(GameObject.Find("FPSController").transform);
```

...with the following code (we just specify that we now look at the centre of the FPSController, where the object **playerMiddle** has been added).

Using Finite State Machines

```
transform.LookAt(GameObject.Find("playerMiddle").transform);
```

... and replace the line...

```
ray.origin = transform.position;
```

... with the following code (this will make sure that the ray is starting 1 meter above the ground so that it can be used to detect objects ahead):

```
ray.origin = transform.position + Vector3.up;
```

Finally, we will, as for the previous clip, need to ensure that the clip for the state **FOLLOW_PLAYER** is looping:

- Please locate the animation **walking** in your project (e.g., perform a search for the word **walking** in the **Project** window).

- Click on it to see its properties in the **Inspector** window.

- Set its attribute **Loop Time** to **true**, as you have done for the previous clip (i.e., by editing the clip). Also set its attribute **Loop Pose** to **true**; this is so that the animation is executed on the same spot. If you would like to see the impact of the attribute **Loop Pause**, you can change this attribute and then preview the animation clip using the window located in the bottom corner of the **Inspector**.

- Apply these changes (i.e., click on the button **Apply** located in the bottom-right corner of the **Inspector** window).

- Play your scene and check that the game works as expected; by moving in front of the NPC and then moving away from him, you should see that the NPC is following you.

> Please note that currently, if the player changes direction too fast, the NPC may lose sight of the player very easily. So, to be more realistic, we could have implemented a vision detection based on a field of view (e.g., 110 degrees). This could be achieved by calculating the dot product between the forward vectors of the player and the NPC and we will cover this concept later in the book.

Next, we will modify the behavior of the NPC to make it more realistic.

- The NPC will not remain idle after losing site of the player.

- The NPC will keep following the player even if it loses sight of the player.

- The NPC will attack the player when it is close (e.g., close combat technique).

First, let's look at the attacking state.

Using Finite State Machines

Please select the object **NPC1**, open the **Animator** window, and modify the **Animator Controller** by creating a Boolean parameter called **withinArmsReach**.

Please modify the **Animator Controller** by creating the following state and transitions (note that you will also need to drag and drop an animation from the **Project** window to the corresponding state):

- State name: **ATTACK_CLOSE_RANGE**; animation = **punching**.

- Transition: from **FOLLOW_PLAYER** to **ATTACK_CLOSE_RANGE**, condition=" **withinArmsReach =true**".

- Transition: from **ATTACK_CLOSE_RANGE** to **FOLLOW_PLAYER**, condition=" **withinArmsReach =false**".

By creating the previous states and transitions, you modified the behavior of the NPC so that it starts attacking the player when it is within arms' reach, and then resumes following the player when it is not within arms' reach.

> Note that you will need to modify the new animation **punching** so that it loops and set its attribute **Loop Time** to true. You will also need to make sure that the attribute **Loop Pause** is set to true for this animation. To do so, you can select the animation in the project window, and **Edit** its properties using the **Inspector** window.

After creating this state and transitions, the **Animator** window should look as follows:

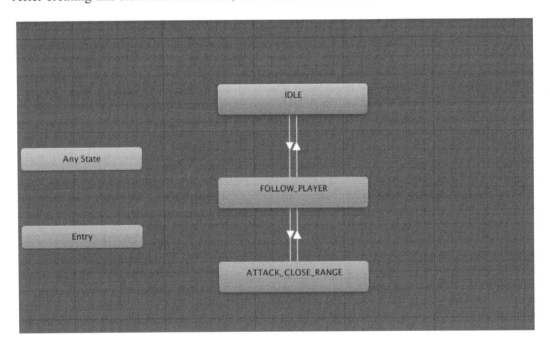

Figure 5-28: The states and transitions for our Animator Controller

Using Finite State Machines

- And the parameters should be listed as follows:

Figure 5-29: Parameters for the Animator Controller

Once this is done, we just need to make sure that the parameter we have just defined (i.e., **withinArmsReach**) is triggered from our script.

- Please open the script **ControlNPCFSM**.

- Add the following code at the beginning of the script (i.e., where other variables are declared and within the class).

```
private float distance;
```

In the previous code, we declare the variable **distance**; it will be employed to detect if the NPC is close to the player.

Add the following code at the beginning of the method **Update** (new code in bold).

```
void Update ()
{
    distance = Vector3.Distance(gameObject.transform.position, GameObject.Find("FPSController").transform.position);
    bool withinReach, closeToPlayer;
    withinReach = (distance < 1.5f);
    anim.SetBool("withinArmsReach", withinReach);
```

In the previous code:

- We calculate the distance between the player and the **NPC**.

- We declare a Boolean variable (**withinReach**) and we then set its value.

- The variable **withinReach** will be true if the distance between the NPC and the player is less than 1.5 meters.

- We then set the parameter for the **Animator Controller** using this Boolean variable.

[231]

Using Finite State Machines

That's about it!

You can now play the scene and check that if you walk in front of the NPC, it will first walk towards you; then, when close enough, the NPC should start to throw punches.

Figure 5-30: Close-range attack from the NPC

MAKING THE NPC SMARTER

At present, when the NPC follows the player and loses sight of the player, it will stop. To make this behavior more realistic, we could modify our game so that the NPC follows the player, and keeps going in his/her direction, even if it has lost sight of the player. So, we will be using the concept of Navmesh. Using a Navmesh, you can ask Unity to compute a path between an object (i.e., usually referred as a Navmesh agent), and a target.

First we will delete the transition from the state **FOLLOW_PLAYER** to the state IDLE, as the NPC will keep following the player.

- Please click on the object **NPC1**.
- Open the **Animator** window.
- Click on the transition from the state **FOLLOW_PLAYER** to the state **IDLE**.
- Press **DELETE** on your keyboard (or *CTRL + DELETE* for Mac users).
- A new window will appear asking you to confirm your choice.

Figure 5-31: Deleting the transition from FOLLOW_PLAYER to IDLE

- Click on **Delete** to confirm that you want to delete this state.

Once this is done, the **Animator** window should look as follows.

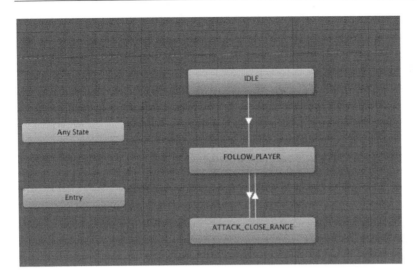

Figure 5-32: The Animator window after deleting the transition

Now that the transition has been deleted, it is time to add "smart" navigation features to our NPC. So, let's add some navigation features to the NPC.

- Please select the NPC (i.e., the object **NPC1**).

- Add a **NavMeshAgent** component to this object (using **Component | Navigation | NavMeshAgent**).

- Using the **Inspector** window, modify the **speed** attribute of this component to **1.0** (i.e., walking speed).

We can now specify the objects that the player can walk on or avoid while pursuing its target; for this purpose, we will use the **Navigation** window.

- Please open the **Navigation** window (**Window | Navigation**).

- Then, using the **Hierarchy** window, select the ground and the wall that you have created.

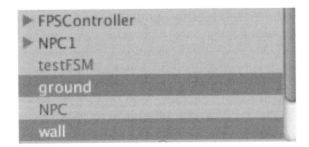

Figure 5-33: Selecting the objects to avoid

Using Finite State Machines

- Once this is done, using the **Navigation** window, in the tab labeled **Object**, click on the option **Navigation Static**.

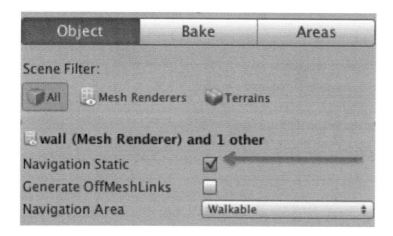

Figure 5-34: Choosing the type of navigation

- If a window labeled **Change Static Flags** appears, select the option **Yes Change Children**.

Figure 5-35: Applying navigation settings to the children

- Once this is done, just click on the **Bake** button located in the bottom-right corner of the **Navigation** window.

Figure 5-36: Baking the scene

- As the baking process is complete, your scene will look different as it includes some of the meshes calculated by Unity to define possible paths for our **NPC**.

[235]

Using Finite State Machines

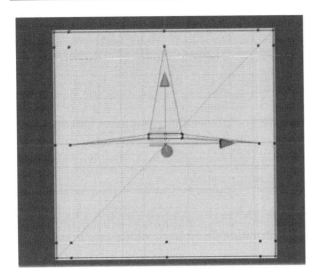

Figure 5-37: Looking at the scene after the baking process is complete

Once this is done, we just need to modify the script **ControlNPCFSM**.

- Please open the script **ControlNPCFSM**.
- Modify the code in the Update method as follows (new code in bold).

```
if (info.IsName("IDLE"))
{
        GetComponent<NavMeshAgent>().Stop();
        print("We are in the IDLE state");
}
else if (info.IsName("ATTACK_CLOSE_RANGE"))
{
        GetComponent<NavMeshAgent>().Stop();
}
else if (info.IsName("FOLLOW_PLAYER"))
{
        GetComponent<NavMeshAgent>().destination =
GameObject.Find("playerMiddle").transform.position;
        GetComponent<NavMeshAgent>().Resume();
        //You can delete the code that was in this section previously
}
```

In the previous code:

- We use the code **GetComponent<NavMeshAgent>().Stop()** so that the NPC stops navigating towards the player whenever it is in the states **IDLE** or **ATTACK_CLOSE_RANGE**.

- If the NPC is in the state **FOLLOW_PLAYER**, we then set the destination (the target) to the player, and then resume the navigation.

Please play the scene, check that after losing sight of the player (e.g., after hiding behind a wall), the NPC still manages to keep track of the player and follow him/her.

ADDING WEAPONS TO THE PLAYER

At this stage, the NPC has a simple behavior whereby it will follow the player once the player is in sight and eventually throw punches when close enough. So we could, at this stage, start to equip our player so that it can use and manage weapons, using the code and prefabs we have created in the previous chapters. For this purpose, and to also keep a backup of the script that we have created in the previous chapter we will perform a series of script duplication.

- Please duplicate the script **ManageWeapons** and call it **ManageWeapons2**.

- Open this script (i.e., **ManageWeapon2**) and change the name of the class within as follows.

- Replace the following code....

```
public class ManageWeapons : MonoBehaviour
```

- ...with this code (changes in bold)...

```
public class ManageWeapons2 : MonoBehaviour
```

- We need to change the name of the class within to avoid conflict with the class **ManageWeapons** that we have already defined in the file **ManageWeapons.cs**.

> If you omit to change the name of the class within after changing the name of the file, Unity may display a message saying "**The namespace global already contains a definition for...**". This message means that this class has already been defined earlier and that there is a potential conflict.

- Please do the same with the scripts **ManageNPC**, **ManageCollisionWithPlayer**, and **Grenade**: duplicate these scripts, add a **2** to the name of the duplicate, and also modify the name of the class within.

- After making these modifications, you should have three additional scripts: **ManageNPC2**, **ManageCollisionWithPlayer2**, and **Grenade2**.

- For clarity, you can add these scripts to a new folder, for example **FSM**, as illustrated on the next figure.

Using Finite State Machines

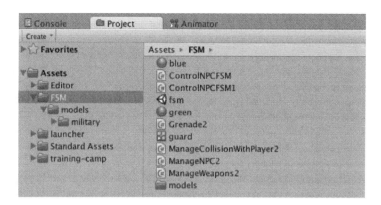

Figure 5-38: Duplicating C# files

- Create a new **RawImage** object (**Game Object | UI | Raw Image**).

- Use the **crosshair** texture that you employed in the last chapter, as a texture for this object.

- Make sure that the crosshair is centered (i.e., displayed in the middle of the screen); for example, you could set its parameters **PosX** and **PosY** to 0.

Once this is done, it is time to add weapons to the player:

- Drag and drop the script **ManageWeapons2** to the object **FirstPersonCharacter**.

- Open this script (**ManageWeapons2**) and replace this code (in the **Update** method):

```
objectTargeted.GetComponent<ManageNPC>().gotHit();
```

...with this code...

```
objectTargeted.GetComponent<ManageNPC2>().gotHit();
```

- Once this is done, select the object **FirstPersonCharacter**, and, using the **Inspector** window, focusing on the component **ManageWeapons2**, set the prefabs for the fields **grenade** and **sparksAtImpact** with the prefabs **grenade** and **smoke**, respectively. You can set these by clicking on the circle to the right of the variable that you need to change, then search for and select the corresponding prefab, as you have done in the previous sections.

Using Finite State Machines

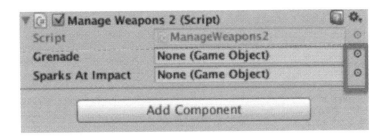

Figure 5-39: Setting the variables grenade and sparksAtImpact from the Inspector

- Finally, create a new **UI | Text** object, rename it **userInfo**, change its **width** to **400**, and set its position to the bottom-left corner of the screen; for example **(-74.5, 150.5, 0)**.

> To move the **Text UI** component you can temporarily switch to the 2D mode, this will display the screen boundaries (i.e., white rectangle) and make it easier to position the **Text UI** component. To activate or deactivate the 2D mode, you can click on the 2D icon located below the tab labeled scene, as described on the next figure.
>
>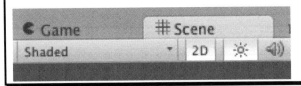

- Drag the audio clip **gunshot** to the object **FirstPersonCharacter**. Also ensure that its option **Play on Awake** is set to false (i.e., after selecting the object **FirstPersonCharacter** and displaying its properties in the **Inspector**).

- Create a new empty object, rename it **launcher**, add it as a child of the object **FirstPersonCharacter**, and set its position to **(0, 0.2, 0)**.

- Play the scene; you should be able to use the different weapons, including the grenades, and to also see the number of ammunitions available.

Next, we will make it possible for the player to collect ammunitions:

- Drag and drop the script **ManageCollisionWithPlayer2** from the project window to the object named **FPSController**.

- Open this script and change its code as follows (new code in bold):

```
void OnControllerColliderHit (ControllerColliderHit hit)
{
     transform.GetChild(0).GetComponent<ManageWeapons2>().manageCollisions(hit);
}
```

- The modification is necessary at this stage, as the other script that manages the weapons has changed name (from **ManageWeapons** to **ManageWeapons2**).

- Locate the prefabs **ammo_auto**, **ammo_grenade**, and **ammo_gun** in your project (i.e., by searching for the word **ammo** in your **Project** window), and drag and drop them several times from your project to the scene, so that it creates new ammos in the scene.

- Please play the scene and check that you can pick-up different types of ammos and that the ammunition levels are updated accordingly.

At this stage, we have successfully recycled the code created in the previous chapter to add weapons to our character. The next phase will now involve applying damage to the NPCs when they are hit.

- Please drag and drop the script **ManageNPC2** on the object **NPC1**.

- Remove the component **ManageNPC** from the object **NPC1** (i.e., right-click on the component and select **Remove Component**).

- Select the object **NPC1** and, using the **Inspector**, set the **smoke** variable for the attached script **ManageNPC2** to the prefab **smoke** (i.e., click on the circle to the right of the variable smoke and search/select the prefab **smoke**).

Last but not list, we need to add colliders to the NPC. At present, the ray casting generated from the player will not detect the NPC because this NPC has no colliders yet. So we will create a collider for the NPC accordingly:

- Please select the object **NPC1**.

- Change its tag to **target**.

- Then select **Component | Physics | Capsule Collider**. This will add a capsule collider to the NPC.

- Modify the attributes of this capsule collider using the **Inspector** window as follows: **Centre (0, 0.82,0)**, **Height (1.75)**, and leave the other options as default.

After making these changes, play the scene, and check that after firing twice or more at the NPC, it disappears.

You may notice, however, that the grenade does not impact on the **NPC**; this is because the grenade object is linked to the script **Grenade.cs**, which needs to be updated.

Using Finite State Machines

- Please select the prefab **grenade** from the **Project** window.
- Deactivate or remove its script component **Grenade.cs**.
- Drag and drop the script **Grenade2.cs** to this object, so that it becomes a component of the **grenade** prefab.
- Set the variable **explosion** for this component (**Grenade2.cs**) to the prefab **explosion**.

Finally, open the script **Grenade2.cs**, and change its code as follows (new code in bold). You can replace the code that was previously within the for loop with the next code.

```
for (int i = 0; i < colliders.Length; i++)
{
        if (colliders [i].gameObject.tag == "target")
        {
          GameObject objectTargeted = colliders [i].gameObject;
          objectTargeted.GetComponent<ManageNPC2>().gotHitByGrenade();
        }
}
```

In the previous script, we check whether the objects within range have a tag called **target**; if this is the case, we then access its script and apply damage.

After making this change, please save your script and test the scene. Using the guns or grenades, you should be able to neutralize the NPC now.

ADDING ANIMATIONS FOR MORE REALISM

Ok. So we can now use our weapons to neutralize the NPC, and it works well; however, we could add more realism to the animations. For example, every time the **NPC** is hit, we could play an animation; when its health is low, we could also play an animation that shows this NPC falling to the ground. All it takes is to create states (e.g., **HIT** or **DIE**), then detect whether the player is hit, and switch to the corresponding states.

So let's get started; first we will create the two additional states:

- Please select the **NPC** (**NPC1**).

- Open the **Animator** window.

- Create two states called **HIT** and **DIE**.

- Create two new parameters: **gotHit** (type = **Trigger**) and **lowHealth** (type = **Boolean**).

> You will notice that we use a **Trigger** variable here (**gotHit**); this is because this parameter will switch back to false after it has been set to true. In other words, this state **HIT** will last for a short period of time and this variable (**gotHit**), because it is true just for a moment, will switch back to its original value right after that. So it makes more sense to use a **Trigger** parameter rather than a Boolean, as the NPC will get hit (this will last for a short moment) but will not remain in this state for a long time.

Please apply the following animations to the states created:

- State = **HIT**; animation = **hit_reaction**.

- State = **DIE**; animation = **dying**.

- You don't need to loop these animations, so no modification of the corresponding clips is necessary for now.

We just need to create the transitions now; please create the following transitions:

- From **HIT** to **DIE**: **lowHealth** = **true**.

- From **HIT** to **ATTACK_CLOSE_RANGE**: **withinArmsReach=true && lowHealth = false**.

Using Finite State Machines

> To include several conditions for a transition, additional transitions can be provided using the + sign in the bottom-right corner of the section **Transition**, in the **Inspector** window.
>
>
>
> Figure 5-40: Adding conditions for transitions
>
> To delete a condition, you can simply click once on the = sign to the right of the variable and then press the − sign located in the bottom-right corner of the window.

- From **Any Sate** to **HIT**: **gotHit**. The state **Any State** is already present in the **Animator** by default, and you can move it by dragging and dropping it to the location of your choice.

- After you have created these states, parameters and transitions, the **Animator** window may look as follows:

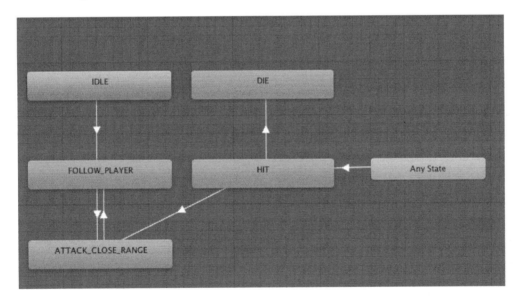

Figure 5-41: New states and transitions

- Once this done, you can check that these transitions work by just playing the scene, displaying both the **Animator** and the **Scene** views simultaneously, and clicking on the parameters and **lowHealth** and then **gotHit** in the **Animator** window.

Using Finite State Machines

- First you can change the **gotHit** variable, the **NPC** should be ducking slightly (as per the next figure); then set the variable **lowHealth** to true, set the variable **gotHit** again and the NPC should start to fall down.

Figure 5-42: The NPC is hit

Figure 5-43: The NPC falls down (part 1)

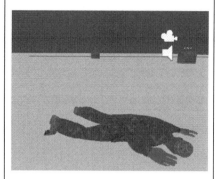

Figure 5-44: The NPC falls down (part 2)

So after checking that these transitions work well, we need to link them to the game. So the process will be to detect when the **NPC** is hit, and set the parameter **gotHit** or **lowHealth** based on its **health**.

- Please open the script **ControlNPCFSM**.

- Add the following lines of code within the class (e.g., at the end of the class, just before the last closing curly bracket).

```
public void setGotHitParameter()
{
    anim.SetTrigger("gotHit");
}

public void setLowHealthParameter()
{
    anim.SetBool("lowHealth",true);
}
```

In the previous code:

- We create two member methods.

- In the first method, we set the **Trigger** variable **gotHit**.

- In the second method, we set the **Boolean** variable **lowHealth** to true.

[245]

Using Finite State Machines

> You may notice that these methods are public, which means that they will be accessible from outside this class, including from other classes.

Next, we will modify the script **manageNPC2.cs**:

- Please open the script **manageNPC2.cs**.
- Modify the methods **gotHit** and **gotHitByGrenade** as follows (new code in bold).

```
public void gotHit()
{
    print ("Got hit by bullet");
    GetComponent<ControlNPCFSM>().setGotHitParameter();
    health -=50;
}
public void gotHitByGrenade()
{
    print ("Got hit by Grenade");
    GetComponent<ControlNPCFSM>().setGotHitParameter();
    health = 0;
}
```

In the previous code:

- We create a method **gotHit**.

- In this method, we access the method **setGotHitParameter** from the script **ControlNPCFSM** that is linked to the same object. This method (i.e., **setGotHitParameter**) will set an animation parameter so that the NPC briefly transitions to the state **HIT**.

- We then decrease the health of the NPC by 50.

- We also update the method **gotHitByGrenade** and proceed as for the previous method except that **health** is set to 0 instead.

Modify the method **Destroy** as follows (new code in bold):

```
public void Destroy()
{
        /*print ("Destroying "+ gameObject.name);
        GameObject lastSmoke = (GameObject) (Instantiate (smoke, transform.position, Quaternion.identity));
        Destroy (lastSmoke,3);
        Destroy(gameObject);*/
        GetComponent<ControlNPCFSM>().setLowHealthParameter();
        Destroy(gameObject, 5);
}
```

In the previous code:

- We comment some of the code (the first 5 lines of the method).

- We access the method **setLowHealthParameter** from the script **ControlNPCFSM**. This is because the script **ControlNPCFSM** is also attached to the NPC (i.e., the object **NPC1**)

- We then destroy the **NPC** after **5** seconds (this should give enough time for the falling animation to be completed).

As you play the scene and use your gun or grenades to neutralize the NPC, you should be able to see the NPC either ducking or falling after being hit by a bullet or a grenade.

APPLYING DAMAGE TO THE PLAYER

In this section, we will give the opportunity for the NPC to also apply damage to the player. If you remember, we have a state called **ATTACK_CLOSE_RANGE**; in this state the NPC throws punches at the player at close range. However, no health points are withdrawn from the player yet. So we will implement this functionality. It will consist in:

- Detecting when the NPC is throwing punches.
- Decreasing a finished amount of health from the player when it's being hit.
- Provide the ability for the player to increase its health by collecting med packs.

So let's get started!

- Please create a new C# script and rename it **ManagePlayerHealth**.
- Add the following code at the beginning of the class (new code in bold).

```
public class ManagePlayerHealth : MonoBehaviour {
int health = 100;
```

Then add the following method (e.g., before the last closing curly bracket):

```
public void decreaseHealth(int healthIncrement)
{
        health -= healthIncrement;
}
```

- Save your script and drag and drop it to the object **FPSController**.
- Open the script **ControlNPCFSM**.
- Add the following code within the **Update** method after the code that deals with the **IDLE** state.

Using Finite State Machines

```
else if (info.IsName("ATTACK_CLOSE_RANGE"))
{
    GetComponent<NavMeshAgent>().Stop();
    if (info.normalizedTime%1.0 >= .98)
    {
        GameObject.Find
("FPSController").GetComponent<ManagePlayerHealth>().decreaseHealth(5);
    }
}
```

In the previous code:

- We check that we are in the state **ATACK_CLOSE_RANGE**.

- We then stop the navigation (i.e., following the player)check if the animation associated to this state is almost complete; and we then call the method **decreaseHealth**. The reason for using the following code…

```
info.normalizedTime%1.0 >= .98
```

… is that, if we don't check that the animation is almost completed, we would decrease the player's health continuously while the animation is played; however, we just want to decrease the player's health after each round of attack (or punch); so we wait until we have reached 98% completion of the animation before we decrease health.

> The variable **info.normalizedTime** returns a number that includes two types of information: the integer part tells us how many times the animation has looped, and the decimal part indicates the percentage of completion of the current loop. So since we are interested in the later (i.e., percentage of completion of the current loop), we use the operator modulo (%) to obtain this value.

We will add a UI component to our scene later, to display the player's health and to check that all works properly.

While this is working, we could also add some challenge in the game by allowing the NPC to shoot at the player. So let's create this behavior.

- Please select the NPC (i.e., the object **NPC1**).

- Open the **Animator** window.

- Create a new state called **SHOOT**.

- Associate this state with the animation **shooting** (i.e., by dragging and dropping the animation on the state or clicking on the circle to the right of the field called **Motion**).

Create the following transitions:

Using Finite State Machines

- From **HIT** to **SHOOT**: **withinArmsReach=false && lowHealth = false**.

- From **SHOOT** to **FOLLOW_PLAYER**: **no conditions.** This means that the state **FOLLOW_PLAYER** will be reached after the animation for the state **SHOOT** is complete.

After performing these changes, the **Animator** window should look as follows.

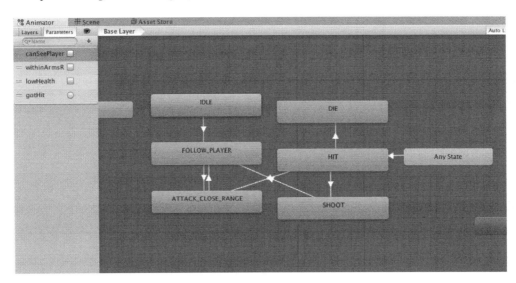

Figure 5-45: The Animator controller with an additional state

After creating these states and transitions, we just need to modify the code for the script **ControlNPCFSM**:

- Please open this script **ControlNPCFSM**.

- Add the following code within the **Update** method just after the code that deals with the state **ATTACK_CLOSE_RANGE**.

[250]

```
else if (info.IsName("HIT"))
{
        GetComponent<NavMeshAgent>().Stop();
}
else if (info.IsName("SHOOT"))
{

        GetComponent<NavMeshAgent>().Stop();
        transform.LookAt(GameObject.Find("playerMiddle").transform);
        if (info.normalizedTime%1.0 >= .98)
        {
                GameObject.Find
("FPSController").GetComponent<ManagePlayerHealth>().decreaseHealth(5);
        }
}
```

In the previous code:

- We check that we are in the state **HIT**; in this case, we make sure that the NPC is not navigating (i.e., that it is stopped).

- We then check for the state **SHOOT**; in this case, we also make sure that the NPC is not navigating (i.e., that it is stopped).

- We then make sure that the NPC is looking in the direction of the player before starting to shoot.

- We finally decrease the health of the player, following the same principle as the one we have used for the state **ATTACK_CLOSE_RANGE**.

Please play and test the scene and make sure that the NPC reacts as predicted (e.g., following the player, or shooting after being hit).

As you check the scene, you may notice that when the NPC is shooting, it has no gun yet in its hand; this is because the animation created did not include the weapon, so we need to add a gun object to this NPC when it is shooting.

So let's add this object:

- You can download a gun object form the following site and link (this model was created by Dennis Haupt):

http://tf3dm.com/3d-model/45-acp-smith-and-wesson-13999.html

- In case this link is not available anymore, it is also included in the resource pack, in the folder **3D models | handgun** (with the permission of the author of this object).

Using Finite State Machines

- Once this done, you can import the folder called **fbx** in Unity. This will include a folder with a prefab for the gun, as well as textures.

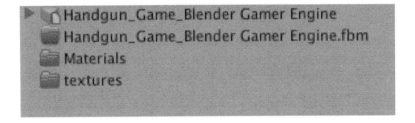

Figure 5-46: Importing a gun object

Once this is done, you can drag and drop the prefab (i.e., the blue box named **Handgun_Game_Blender Gamer Engine**) on the object **NPC1**, so that it becomes a child of the NPC.

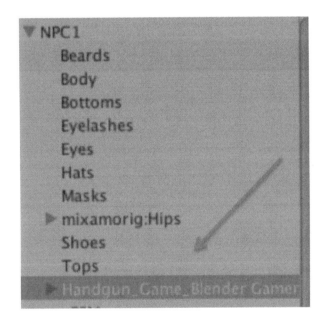

Figure 5-47: Adding the gun as a child of the NPC

We can then adjust its **Transform** settings as follows:

- Position **(0.115, 1.211, 0.759)**.
- Rotation **(0, 90, 0)**.
- Scale **(0.2, 0.2, 0.2)**.

Using Finite State Machines

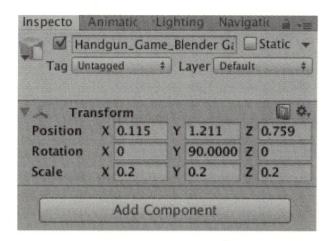

Figure 5-48: Adjusting the transform properties of the gun

- In the **Hierarchy** window, rename this object **hand_gun**.

Figure 5-49: Adding a gun to the NPC

Once this is done, you should see that the gun appears in front of the NPC in the **Scene** view. You can check that the gun is in the right position when the NPC is shooting by doing the following:

- Select the object **NPC1**.

- Focus on this object (*SHIFT + S*).

- Play the scene.

- Open the **Animator** window (you can first press **CTRL + 1** to switch to the **Scene** view and then use your mouse to select the **Animator** window).

[253]

Using Finite State Machines

- Set the variables **lowHealth** and **withinArmsReach** to **false**, and then set the variable **gotHit**.

- Observe the object **NPC1** in the scene view; it should look like the following picture.

Figure 5-50: Positioning the gun

Next, we need to enable this object only when the NPC is shooting:

- Open the script **ControlNPCFSM**.

- Add the following code at the beginning of the class.

```
private GameObject gun;
```

- Then add the following code to the method **Start**.

```
gun = GameObject.Find("hand_gun");
gun.active = false;
```

Finally, add the following code to the **Update** method (new code in bold).

[254]

Using Finite State Machines

```
else if (info.IsName("SHOOT"))
{
    GetComponent<NavMeshAgent>().Stop();
    if(anim.IsInTransition(0)&&
anim.GetNextAnimatorStateInfo(0).IsName("FOLLOW_PLAYER")) gun.active = false;
    else gun.active = true;
    transform.LookAt(GameObject.Find("playerMiddle").transform);
    if (info.normalizedTime%1.0 >= .98)
    {
        GameObject.Find
("FPSController").GetComponent<ManagePlayerHealth>().decreaseHealth(5);
    }
}
```

In the previous code that is highlighted in bold:

- We check that the **Animator Controller** is transitioning and that it is transitioning to the state called **FOLLOW_PLAYER** from the state **SHOOT**.

- When this is verified, we just deactivate the gun so that it can't be seen.

- The method **GetNextAnimatorStateInfo()** provides the next state to be reached in the first layer (hence the parameter 0). We then use the method **IsName** to obtain its name.

The last things we need to do are to:

- Display the player's health and number of lives.

- Reload the level when health levels are low.

- Increase the health levels when the player collects ammunitions.

- Decrease the number of lives by one.

So we will modify the script **ManagePlayerHealth** accordingly.

- Open the script **ManagePlayerHealth**.

- Add this code at the beginning of the class (i.e., where other variables are declared).

```
int nbLives = 3;
```

- Modify the method **decreaseHealth** as follows:

Using Finite State Machines

```
public void decreaseHealth(int healthIncrement)
{
     print ("Decreasing health by "+ healthIncrement);
     health -= healthIncrement;
     if (health <=0) restartLevel();
}
```

- Then add the following methods to the script (at the end of the class):

```
public void increaseHealth(int healthIncrement)
{
    health += healthIncrement;
}
public void restartLevel()
{
    nbLives--;
    health = 100;
    Application.LoadLevel(Application.loadedLevel);
}
public void Awake()
{
   DontDestroyOnLoad(transform.gameObject);
}
```

In the previous code:

- We create a method that increases the health of the player.
- We create a method that restarts the current level after the player has lost a life.
- We create a method that ensures that the object linked to this script (the player) is persistent. In other word, even if the scene is reloaded, this object will not be destroyed. This means that the information on health levels and the number of lives is also kept whenever the scene is reloaded.

Finally, add the following code in the **Start** function (new code in bold):

```
void Start ()
{
     GameObject [] clones = new GameObject [2];
     clones = GameObject.FindGameObjectsWithTag("Player");
     if (clones.Length > 1) Destroy (clones[1]) ;
}
```

In the previous code:

- As we will restart, the level will already include an object called **FPSController**.

- As a result there will be two of these objects (i.e., since the previous one will be kept using the method **DontDestroyOnLoad**).

- So we detect whether there is a duplicate and remove one of them.

- Finally we set the health to **100**.

After this, we just need to create and add health packs:

- Please duplicate the prefab **ammo_gun**.

- Rename the duplicate prefab **health_pack**.

- Create a tag **health_pack** and apply it to this prefab.

- Drag and drop this prefab to the scene.

- This should create a new object called **health_pack** and an object within called **ammo_label**, as described on the next figure.

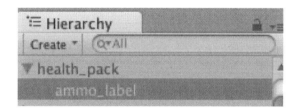

Figure 5-51: Identifying the label for the health pack

- Click on the **ammo_label** object.

- Using the **Inspector** window, change its text to **Health Pack**.

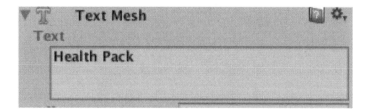

Figure 5-52: Changing the label of the health pack

- Then, so that these changes are applied to the prefab, you can select this object and, using the **Inspector** window, click on the **Apply** button located in the top right corner of the screen, as illustrated on the next figure.

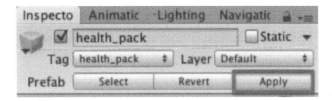

Figure 5-53: Applying changes to the prefab

We will now modify the scripts so that, upon collision with health packs, health levels are increased:

- Please open the script **ManageWeapons2.cs**.
- Add the following code at the end of the method **manageCollisions**.

```
if (tagOfTheOtherObject =="health_pack")
{
    GameObject.Find
("FPSController").GetComponent<ManagePlayerHealth>().increaseHealth(50);
    Destroy (hit.collider.gameObject);

}
```

- Modify the method **increaseHealth** in the script **ManagePlayerHealth** as follows (new code in bold).

```
public void increaseHealth(int healthIncrement)
{
    health += healthIncrement;
    if (health > 100) health = 100;
}
```

- You can also check your health levels by adding the following code to the **Update** method in the same script (i.e., **ManagePlayerHealth**).

```
print ("Health is: " + health);
```

- Please test your scene, and check that, after being hit by a bullet and having collected a health pack, your health is increased (i.e., you can check the **Console** window).

> Before testing the game, make sure that the variable **gotHit** is set to false in the **Animator** window.

Last but not list, we will display the health and life information onscreen:

- Create two new **UI | Text** objects by duplicating the object **userInfo** twice.
- Rename the duplicates **healthInfo** and **livesInfo**.

- Place them just above the **userInfo GameObject** (you can temporarily switch to the 2D view to see and move these objects accordingly, select one of them, and focus on it by pressing *CTRL + F*).

> To switch between the 2D/3D modes while the **Scene** view is active, you can just press the key **2** on your keyboard.

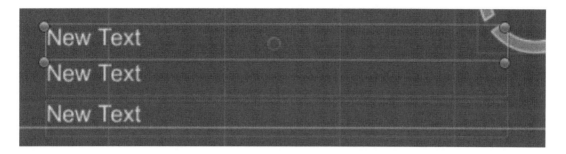

Figure 5-54: Adjusting the position of the UI Text objects

Then, we just need to modify the script **ManagePlayerHealth**.

- Please open the script **ManagePlayerHealth**.
- Add the following code at the beginning of the script.

```
using UnityEngine.UI;
```

- Modify the method **Update** as follows:

```
void Update ()
{
    print ("Health" + health);
    GameObject.Find ("healthInfo").GetComponent<Text>().text = "Health: " + health;
    GameObject.Find ("livesInfo").GetComponent<Text>().text = "Lives: " + nbLives;
}
```

> It is usually good practice not to use **GameObject.Find** or any time-consuming statements in the **Update** method. So you could, but this is only optional here, modify this code by creating a global variable that points to the object **livesInfo**. Then, you could initialize this **object** using the method **GameObject.Find** in the **Start** function; finally, you could use this object (with no use of the method **GameObject.Find**) in the **Update** function.

- You can now play the scene and check that the number of lives and health levels are displayed onscreen.

Using Finite State Machines

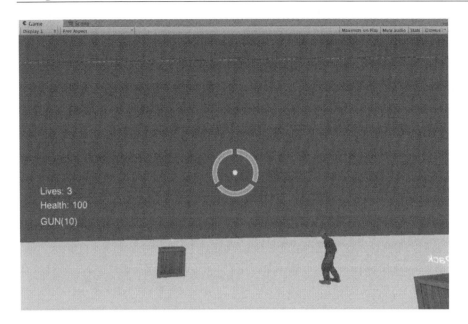

Figure 5-55: Displaying health levels and number of lives.

USING DOT PRODUCTS FOR MORE ACCURACY

Now, as you play and test the scene, you should see that the NPC will follow you whenever you walk pass him. However, the sight detection, as it is, may not be as accurate as it could be. This is because, at present, the field of view of this NPC is extremely narrow, as we expect to detect only objects at a 0 degree angle from him; not only is this not accurate, but it can cause some undesirable effects and behaviors. However, we can correct this easily using a more realistic field of view. For this we will use a bit of algebra, that is, using the dot product. The **dot product** is a mathematical concept that basically tells us about the angle between two vectors; so to mimic the field of view of the NPC, we would like to know whether the player is in front of the NPC +/- several degrees, as illustrated on the next figure.

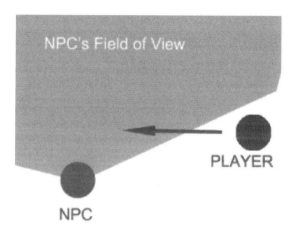

Figure 5-56: Illustrating the player's field of view

The definition of a dot product between two vectors is the product of their magnitude multiplied by the cosine of the angle between these vectors. In practical terms, we multiply the two vectors; however, to do so, we need to consider whether they are in the same direction. So the cosine will provide us with the projection of one of the vectors on the other one and multiply this projection then by the magnitude of the other vector.

> The dot product effectively tells us about the angle between these vectors and to what extent they are aligned; for example, a positive dot product indicates that the angle between the two vectors is between -90 and 90 degrees, a null dot product indicates that they are perpendicular to each other.

The formula is as follows:

D = |v1| x |v2| x Cos (alpha).

Where:

- D is the dot product between the two vectors.
- Alpha is the angle between the two vectors.

In Unity, the built-in classes make it easier to use the dot product, as demonstrated below:

```
Vector3 v1 = new Vector3 (1.0f,1.0f,1.0f);
Vector3 v2 = new Vector3 (-2.0f,-2.0f,-2.0f);
float productOfV1AndV2 = Vector3.Dot(v1,v2);
```

- Line 1: the vector v1 is created.
- Line 2: the vector v2 is created.
- Line 3: the dot product of these vectors is calculated.
- In this case, the dot product is -2; so we know that the angle between the vectors is between -90 and 90 degrees.

It would be great, however, to know more about the direction of these vectors, and more importantly if they are aligned or pointing in the same direction. For this purpose, we can normalize these vectors first (i.e., reduce their magnitude to 1). This way, if they are in the exact same direction, the dot product will be 1; and if they are in the opposite direction, the dot product will be -1. This is because when we calculate the dot product, if the magnitudes of both vectors are 1, the dot product will be equal to the cosine of the angle between these two. Because the cosine is equal to one if the angle is 0 and -1 if the angle is 180, it is now easier to check if these vectors are aligned. In Unity, we could do this as follows:

```
Vector3 v1 = new Vector3 (1.0f,1.0f,1.0f);
Vector3 v2 = new Vector3 (-2.0f,-2.0f,-2.0f);
float productOfV1AndV2 = Vector3.Dot(v1.normalized,v2. normalized);
```

- The first two lines are similar to the previous code.
- Line3: we calculate the dot product of these vectors, after they have been normalized; in this case, we will find that the dot product equals -1 (i.e., vectors are pointing to opposite directions).

If we call the field of view **alpha**, knowing whether the NPC is in the field of view is equivalent to know whether the angle determined by the direction of the NPC (V1 on the next diagram) and the vector that points at the player from the NPC (V2 in the next diagram) is comprised between -alpha/2 and alpha/2. So for a field of view of 90 degrees, the angle defined by V1 and V2 should be comprised between -45 degrees and +45 degrees. This is explained on the next diagram. As the player enters the NPCs' field of view, the vector V2 will rotate counterclockwise.

Using Finite State Machines

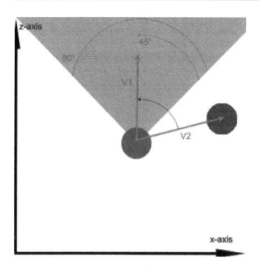

Figure 5-57: Illustrating the player entering the NPC's field of view

So, as described on the previous diagram, and knowing that cosine (45) is approximately 0.7 and that cosine (-45) is approximately also 0.7, we know that the player is in the field of view of the NPC if the angle between V1 and V2 is between -45 degrees and +45 degrees, or, in a similar way, if the cosine of the angle between the vectors V1 and V2 is comprised between 0.7 and 1. This is because when the player is on the right border of the field of view, the angle between V1 and V2 is -45° (i.e., cosine = 0.7).

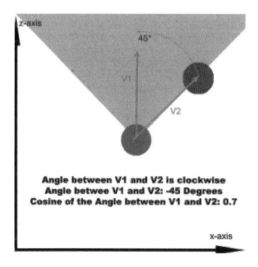

Figure 5-58: the player enters the right boundary of the field of view

- When the player is in front of the NPC, the angle between V1 and V2 is 0 (Cosine = 1).

- When the player is on the left border of the field of view, the angle between V1 and V2 is 45° (Cosine = 0.7). So effectively, when the NPC is in the field of view, the Cosine of the angle will vary between 0.7 and 1.

[263]

Using Finite State Machines

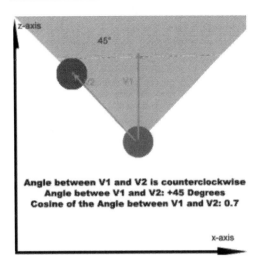

Figure 5-59: Exiting the NPC's field of view

- The field of view could be any number of your choice. We have arbitrarily chosen 90 degrees to simulate the horizontal field of view for some humans, but you could, if you wished, increase it to 100 degrees or more.

- Now that we have clarified the calculation of the **Cosine**, let's see how we can find the vectors V1 and V2.

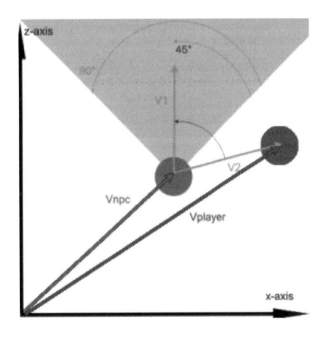

Figure 5-60: Calculating V2

- V1 is the direction of the NPC. This vector originates (on the previous diagram) from the NPC and is going in the direction of the positive z-axis. V2 is determined by the position

[264]

of both the NPC and the Player. Let's see how. As you can see on the next diagram, V2, Vnpc and Vplayer form a triangle. Vnpc is the vector for the position of the NPC. It starts at the origin of the coordinate system. Vplayer is the vector for the position of the NPC and, as for the previous vector, it starts at the origin of the coordinate system. If we operate a loop from the origin of the coordinate system, we can go from the origin of the coordinate system to the NPC by following the vector Vnpc, we follow the vector V2 (in reverse: from the head to the tail), and then following the vector Vplayer (in reverse: from the head to the tail). So we could say that: **Vnpc + V2-Vplayer = 0**; in other words, by following Vnpc, then V2 in reverse and Vplayer in reverse, we end up at the same point. Following this, we can then say that: V2 = -Vnpc + Vplayer (we add -V2 to both sides of the previous equation). This is how we can calculate V2.

- Normalizing the vectors: so at this stage, we know V1 and V2 and we just need to calculate the dot product between these to have an idea of the cosine of the angle. However, if you remember the definition of a dot product, the cosine of this angle equals the dot product only if the magnitude of the vectors is 1, or in other words, if these vectors have been normalized. Normalizing can be done easily in Unity as each vector can access the function/method **normalized** which returns a normalized version accordingly.

- At this stage, we have two normalized vectors (magnitude equals 1) and we need to calculate the cosine of the angle defined by them. You will notice that so far, we have been using degrees for angles (FOV=90°). However, the function that calculates the Cosine in Unity only takes Radians (and not Degrees) as parameters. So we will need to convert our angle in radians first before the cosine can be calculated. This can be done using the function **Mathf.Deg2Rad** in Unity.

- Now we have an angle expressed in radians and we can calculate the dot product of the normalized versions of V1 and V2. That's great! Bearing in mind that when the player is on the right boundary of the field of view, the angle between V1 and V2 is -45° (Cosine = 0.7), when the player is in front of the NPC, the angle between V1 and V2 is 0 (Cosine = 1), and that when the player is on the left border of the field of view, the angle between V1 and V2 is 45° (Cosine = 0.7), we effectively know that for the NPC to detect the player (or the player to enter the Field of View of the NPC), the cosine of the angle between V1 and V2 should be comprised between 0.7 and 1.

Now that the principle of dot products is clear, we could apply it to our own code, as follows:

- Please open the script **ControlNPCFSM**.

- Please add the following code at the beginning of the script.

```
public Vector3 direction;
public bool isInTheFieldOfView;
public bool noObjectBetweenNPCAndPlayer = false;
```

- Add the following code at the beginning of the **Update** method.

Using Finite State Machines

```
direction   =   (GameObject.   Find("FPSController").transform.position   -
transform.position).normalized;
isInTheFieldOfView = (Vector3.Dot(transform.forward.normalized, direction) >
.7);
Debug.DrawRay(transform.position, direction * 100, Color.green);
Debug.DrawRay(transform.position, transform.forward * 100, Color.blue);
if (Physics.Raycast(transform.position, direction * 100, out hit))
{
        if (hit.collider.gameObject.tag == "Player") noObjectBetweenNPCAndPlayer
= true;
        else noObjectBetweenNPCAndPlayer = false;
}
if (noObjectBetweenNPCAndPlayer && isInTheFieldOfView)
{
        anim.SetBool ("canSeePlayer", true);
        transform.LookAt(GameObject.Find("playerMiddle").transform);

}
else anim.SetBool ("canSeePlayer", false);
```

In the previous code:

- We set the variable **direction** to be the direction between the player and the NPC.

- We then set the variable **isInTheFieldOfView** to true if the dot product between the direction of the NPC and the vector direction (i.e., direction if the NPC had to look at the player) is between .7 and 1. Note that we use normalized vectors, so the dot product can only be between -1 and 1.

- We also cast two rays that you will be able to see in the scene view: one in the NPC's direction (i.e., forward), and the other one from the NPC and toward the player.

- Once this is done, we cast a ray between the NPC and the player.

- So if this ray collides with the NPC object, we know that there is nothing between the NPC and the player.

- Finally, if there are no objects between the NPC and the player and the player is in the field of view, we set the animation parameter to true, otherwise it is set to false.

Finally, we can also comment the previous code that was used to detect if the player was in the line of sight, as follows, within the **Update** method.

Using Finite State Machines

```
/*
objectInSight = "";
Debug.DrawRay (ray.origin, ray.direction * 100, Color.red);
if (Physics.Raycast(ray.origin, ray.direction * 100, out hit))
{
        objectInSight = hit.collider.gameObject.tag;
        print ("Object in Sight" + objectInSight);
        if (objectInSight == "Player")
        {
                anim.SetBool ("canSeePlayer",true);
                print ("Just saw the Player");
        }
}
*/
```

You can now play the scene; you can look at the **Scene** view and the **Game** view simultaneously if you wish; as you move the player around, look at the two rays originating from the NPC and the angle between them, as illustrated on the next figure.

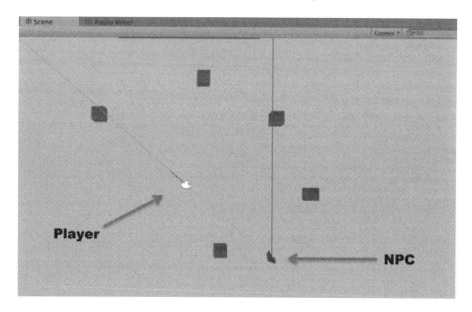

- Once you reach the 45-degree angle within the NPC's field of view, the NPC will start to follow you.

So, as you can see, simple algebra can be very handy to solve some challenges paused by game design, and dot products are extremely useful in the case of fields of view.

Using Finite State Machines

ADDING A SCREEN FLASH WHEN THE PLAYER IS HIT

As the NPC can target us, it would be great to add feedback as to when we have been hit by the NPC. One common ways to do this is to add a screen flash; that is, a brief moment when the screen flashes to red. There are many ways to achieve this effect, and one of them is to create a texture or color material and quickly fade its alpha (i.e., transparency) value from opaque to fully transparent.

So here, we will achieve this effect using a **UI Image** component.

- Please create a new **UI | Image** object.
- Rename it **screenFlash**.

Please change its **Rect Transform** properties as follows:

- Type: **Stretch/Stretch**.
- Left: **0**.
- Top: **0**.
- Pos Z: **0**.
- Right: **1**.
- Bottom: **1**.

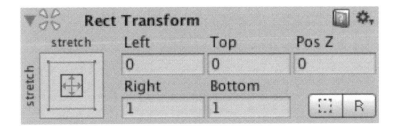

Figure 5-61: Modifying the properties of the UI Image

- This will ensure that the image fills the screen.
- Please change its **color** to **red** and its **transparency to 100%** (Alpha = 0). The transparency attribute is marked as **A** on the second figure.

[268]

Using Finite State Machines

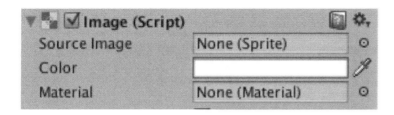

Figure 5-62: Changing the color and transparency of the UI Image (part 1)

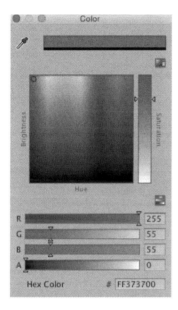

Figure 5-63: Changing the color and transparency of the UI Image (part 2)

We will now modify the script **ManagePlayerHealth** so that this red screen appears briefly whenever the player is hit.

- Please open the script **ManagePlayerHealth** and add the following code at the beginning.

```
public float alpha;
public bool screenFlashBool;
```

- Then add the following code at the end of the method **decreaseHealth**.

```
screenFlash();
```

- Add the following to the **Start** method.

```
alpha = 0;
GameObject.Find("screenFlash").GetComponent<Image>().color = new Color
(1,0,0,alpha);
screenFlashBool = false;
```

- In the previous code, we set the color of the **screenFlash** object, using the RGB code (i.e., Red = 1, Green = 0, Blue = 0) to red and its alpha value to 0 (i.e., transparent). The RGB values are normalized here; this means that the values will range between 0 and 1;

- Add the following method at the end of the class:

```
private void screenFlash ()
{
      screenFlashBool = true;
      alpha = 1.0f;
      print ("Screen Flash");
}
```

- In the previous code, we specify that the screen flash effect should start, and we then set the **alpha** value of the **screenFlash** object to **1** (i.e., it will initially be opaque and progressively become transparent).

- Finally, add the following code to the **Update** method.

```
if (screenFlashBool)
{
      alpha -= Time.deltaTime;
      GameObject.Find("screenFlash").GetComponent<Image>().color = new Color
(1,0,0,alpha);
      if (alpha <=0)
      {
            screenFlashBool = false;
            alpha = 0;
      }
}
```

In the previous code:

- We decrease the alpha value of the **screenFlash** object.

- When this value has reached **0** (i.e., totally transparent) the screen flash effect can be stopped.

- Please save your code and check that the screen flash appears whenever the player has been hit.

Using Finite State Machines

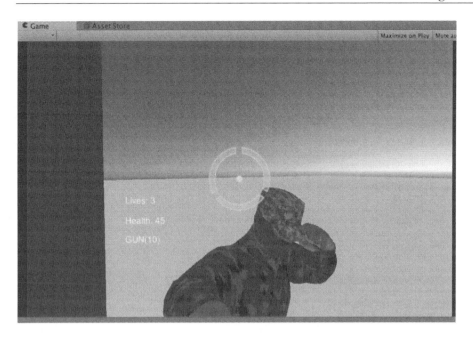

Figure 5-64: The player is about to get hit by the NPC

Figure 5-65: The screen flash is displayed when the player is hit

So all seems to work well, we can now save our NPC and create a prefab with it, so that it can be reused at a later stage.

- Please drag and drop the object **NPC1** to the project window.

- Rename the prefab **npc_guard**.
- In the **Hierarchy** window, the object **NPC1** should turn into an object called **npc_guard**.
- Drag and drop the prefab **npc_guard** several times in the scene, and test the game.

CREATING NEW PREFABS

Now that all works well, we could create prefabs with some of the objects that we may reuse later on.

We can then create groups of objects:

- Please rename the **Canvas** object **UI** (assuming that you have created all the UI objects within this canvas); Unity usually includes all UI elements within the same canvas object by default.

- Create a prefab with the object **UI** (by dragging and dropping this object to the **Project** window) so that its elements can be reused in a different scene.

- You can also create a new prefab based on the object **FPSController** (its default name will be **FPSController**; please keep this name for the prefab for now). When you do so, make sure that you create this prefab in the folder called Assets or another folder of your choice, so that you can identify and use this particular prefab easily later on.

> If you have made any modifications to the objects **npc_guard**, you can update its corresponding prefab also.

After playing the scene you may notice that the gun may always be active for some of the NPCs; this may be, in part, due to the fact that, when we created our scene initially, there was only one NPC and also only one gun; so the following code made perfect sense:

```
gun = GameObject.Find("hand_gun");
```

However, as we add more NPCs, there will inevitably be more characters, hence more objects with the name **hand_gun**. So we need to make sure that when we activate or deactivate a gun, the object that we manipulate is in this case a child of the NPC to which the script **ControlNPCFSM** is attached. To do so, we just need to replace the previous code, in the script ControlNPCFSM, with the following code:

```
gun = transform.Find("hand_gun").gameObject;
```

In the previous code, we specifically target the object named **hand_gun**, which is a child of the NPC to which the script is attached.

Please modify the script, save it, and test the scene.

LEVEL ROUNDUP

In this chapter, we have learned how to create and manage a finite state machine. We became more comfortable with creating states, transitions, and parameters. We managed to create NPCs that behave relatively realistically and to control their behaviors through our scripts. So, again, we have covered considerable ground to produce a relatively interesting scenario. In the next section, we will create a last level where we put all these skills together.

Checklist

You can consider moving to the next stage if you can do the following:

- Create an **Animator Controller**.
- Create states, parameters, and transitions.
- Add animations to a state and configure this animation.
- Manage a state from a script.
- Detect, from a script, if a state is transitioning.

Quiz

Now, let's check your knowledge! Please answer the following questions (the answers are included one the next page).

1. It is possible to duplicate an Animator Controller using the keys *CTRL + D*.

2. The following code will change the value of a Boolean parameter for an animation.

```
SetParameter("canSeePlayer", true).
```

3. The variable type **AnimatorInfo** can be used to provide information about a specific animation.

4. By default, within an Animation Controller, a Boolean parameter is set to false.

5. If the **Animator** linked to this script is in the state **FOLLOW_PLAYER**, the following code will display the message **We are in the FOLLOW_PLAYER Mode**.

```
private Animator anim;
private AnimatorStateInfo info;
anim = GetComponent<Animator>();
info = anim.GetCurrentAnimatorStateInfo(0);
if (info.IsName("FOLLOW_PLAYER")) print ("We are in the FOLLOW_PLAYER Mode");
```

6. When using finite state machines, it is possible to have two states active at the same time.

7. In Mecanim, for a transition to occur between two states, a condition always needs to be defined.

8. The following code will stop the movement of a **NavMeshAgent**.

```
GetComponent<NavMeshAgent>().Stop();
```

9. The following code, provided that the script is linked to an object that includes a **NavMeshAgent**, will display the distance between the NPC and its destination.

```
print (GetComponent<NavMeshAgent>().remainingDistance);
```

10. Complete the following code so that we can test if the **Animator** is transitioning and that the next state is **GoBacktoStart**.

```
if(anim.IsInTransition(0)&& MISSING CODE)
```

Solutions to the Quiz

1. TRUE.
2. FALSE.
3. TRUE.
4. TRUE.
5. TRUE.
6. FALSE.
7. FALSE.
8. TRUE.
9. TRUE.
10.

```
if(anim.IsInTransition(0)&&
anim.GetNextAnimatorStateInfo(0).IsName("GoBacktoStart")))
```

Challenge 1

Now that you have managed to complete this chapter and that you have improved your skills, you could use these to improve the flow of your game. So for this challenge, you will be creating a new type of NPC that will behave as follows:

- It will be similar to the first NPC (guard).
- It will not move from its spot.
- It will shoot at the player when it sees him/her.

Challenge 2

In this challenge, you can create another type of NPC; this NPC will do the following:

- Always look for the player using a **NavMeshAgent**.
- Shoot at the player when the player is in sight and the distance between them is less than 10 meters.
- All other aspects of its behavior are the same as the **guard**.

6
PUTTING IT ALL TOGETHER

In this section we will put all the skills that we have learned to create a fully functional level with the following features:

- The player has three lives.
- The player will then need to collect 10 objects in the scene to win.
- The player will need to avoid or neutralize NPCs.
- The level will include a combination of safe and dangerous areas.
- Ammos will be present in places and possibly re-spawn when the player runs low on ammunitions.
- NPCs will be present at the start of the game.
- The player wins if he/she has collected all 10 objects.
- The player will lose if s/he has no lives left.

SETTING-UP THE ENVIRONMENT MANUALLY

To setup the environment, we will generate an indoor scene using the duplication techniques that were covered in the very first book in the series. We will create a box, texture it, and duplicate it to generate the outline of a simple maze.

- Please save the previous scene with a name of your choice.

- Create a new scene and rename it (i.e., save it as) **gameLevel**, or any other name of your choice.

- Create a new box, rename it **ground**, set its scale property to **(100, 1, 100)** and its position to **(0, 0, 0)**.

- You can also create a material for the ground if you wish or create and apply a blue **Material** to this object.

- You can also change the **Light** settings for the scene (**Window | Lighting**) or add a new light of your choice.

Next, we will create an object that will be used to instantiate the walls.

- Please create a new cube.

- Rename it **wall**.

- Set its **scale** property to **(10, 3, 10)**.

- Set its **y** position to **2**, so that it appears just above the ground.

- You can also create and apply a red **Material** to this object.

Once this is done, you can duplicate this shape several times and move the duplicates to achieve a layout similar to the following one (viewed from above).

Putting it all together

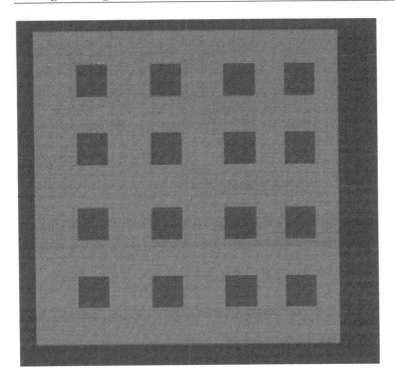

Figure 6-1: Above view of the maze

- You can deactivate the main camera.

- Drag and drop the prefab **UI** to the scene. This prefab includes UI elements that display health and ammo information too.

- Drag and drop the prefab **FPSController** (the one you have just created in the previous scene and stored in the **Assets** folder) to this scene. As you look for this prefab, you will find two prefabs with the same name (the original built-in prefab and the one you have modified in the previous chapters). So, to make sure you have the right one, select it and check in the **Inspector** window that it includes two scripts **ManagePlayerHealth** and **ManageCollisionWithPlayer2**.

- Play the scene and check that you can see your ammunitions and also use your weapons.

Putting it all together

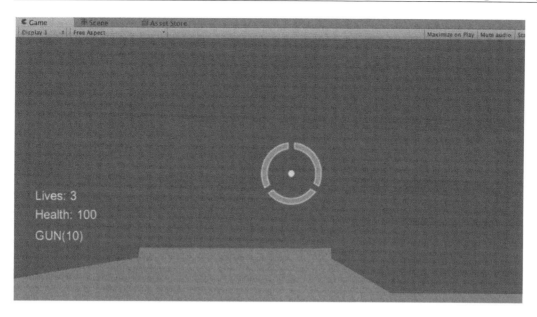

Figure 6-2: Testing the new scene made from prefabs

- Then drag and drop some ammunitions and health packs prefabs in the scene.

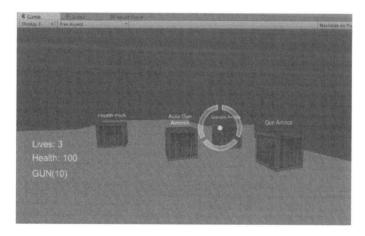

Figure 6-3: Adding med packs to the scene

Next, we can start to add NPCs by dragging one or several **npc_guard** prefabs in the scene. You can also rotate them so that they face a particular direction. To increase the difficulty of this level, you can place these guards near the ammunitions, for example.

Putting it all together

Next, we will compute the Navmesh information so that our NPC can navigate properly:

- Select all the ammos, med packs, the walls and the ground in the scene.
- Switch to the **Navigation** window.
- Check the box **Navigation Static**.

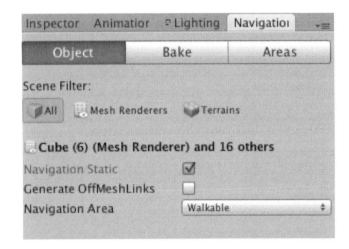

Figure 6-4: Setting navigation attributes

- And click on the button **Bake** located in the bottom-right corner of the **Navigation** window. If a window asks whether you would like to "modify the children", please click on **Yes**.
- Once the baking process is complete, the scene view should look as follows:

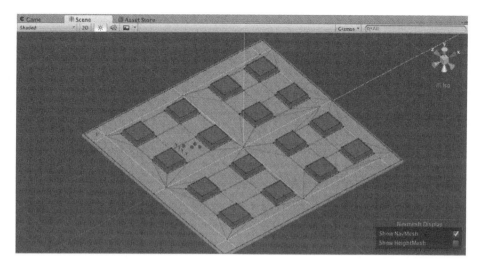

So now, we just need to:

- Add objects to collect.
- Count them as we collect them.
- Load the **Win** scene when the player has collected all of them.
- Load the **Lose** scene when the player has been killed (i.e., nbLives = 0).

First let's create two scenes: one for when the player wins and the other one for when the player loses.

- Please save the current scene.
- Create a new scene and rename it **loseScene** (e.g., using **File | Save Scene As...**).
- Add a simple **UI Text** element that says "**Too Bad, you've just lost**".
- Adjust the size and position of this object so that it is displayed onscreen.
- Save the scene.
- Copy this scene (using the **Inspector** window), rename the duplicate **winScene**, and change the **UI Text** object so that it displays **"Congratulations"**. To look for all the scenes in the project, you can use the key words **t:scene** in the **Project**'s search window. Then you can duplicate the scene by selecting it and then pressing CTRL + D. You can rename and open the duplicate scene to modify it.
- Once this is done, save the scene and go back to the **gameLevel** scene.
- Add this scene, as well as the **win** and **lose** scenes to the build settings (**File | Build Settings**).

Putting it all together

Once this is done, we just need to gain access to these scenes from our scripts.

- Please open the script **ManagePlayerHealth**.
- Modify the script as follows (new code in bold).

```
public void restartLevel()
{
    nbLives --;
    health = 100;
    if (nbLives >=0) Application.LoadLevel(Application.loadedLevel);
    else Application.LoadLevel("lostScene");
}
```

Next, we will work on adding objects to collect and count them.

- Create a sphere that will need to be collected by the player.
- Create a tag called **pick_me** (if not done yet), and apply it to this sphere.
- Add a color to this sphere if you wish.
- Duplicate this sphere nine times and move the duplicates in different locations (i.e., far apart from each other)

Then we will modify the scripts **ManageWeapons2**.

- Open this script.
- Create a private integer variable called **score**.
- Initialize it to 0 in the **Start** method.
- Modify the method **manageCollision** as follows (i.e., add the following code at the end of the method).

```
if (tagOfTheOtherObject =="pick_me")
{
    Destroy (hit.collider.gameObject);
    score++;
    if (score >=9) Application.LoadLevel("winScene");
}
```

Last but not least, please make sure that you have added the new scenes **gameLevel**, **winScene** and **lostScene** to the build settings (if it has no been done yet), so that they can be loaded accordingly.

Please save this script (i.e., **ManageWeapons2**) and test the game; you should see that after collecting all the spheres, the scene **winScene** will be displayed.

This being said, you may also notice that there is an error message in the Console window ("**Object reference not set to an object**"). This error may occur in the scripts **ManageWeapons2** and **ManagePlayerHealth**. This is due to the fact that the player is not destroyed before the win scene is loaded.

So we will modify these scripts as follows.

- Please open the script **ManageWeapons2**.
- Replace the following line in the **Update** method....

```
GameObject.Find("userInfo").GetComponent<Text>().text = weaponName[currentWeapon]+ "("+ammos[currentWeapon]+")";
```

... with this code...

```
if(GameObject.Find("userInfo")!=null)
GameObject.Find("userInfo").GetComponent<Text>().text = weaponName[currentWeapon]+ "("+ammos[currentWeapon]+")";
```

- Then open the script **ManagePlayerHealth**.
- Replace the following code...

```
GameObject.Find ("healthInfo").GetComponent<Text>().text = "Health: " + health;
GameObject.Find ("livesInfo").GetComponent<Text>().text = "Lives: " + nbLives;
```

...with this code...

```
if (GameObject.Find ("healthInfo") !=null) GameObject.Find ("healthInfo").GetComponent<Text>().text = "Health: " + health;
if (GameObject.Find ("livesInfo") != null) GameObject.Find ("livesInfo").GetComponent<Text>().text = "Lives: " + nbLives;
```

You can now test your game again and ensure that no errors appear in the **Console** window after you win the game.

Putting it all together

SETTING-UP THE ENVIRONMENT THROUGH SCRIPTING

This section is optional; however, it may be useful if you would like to generate environments from your script; as we have seen in the previous section, you can set-up your environment manually by creating walls and moving them in particular locations; however, there are times when you would like to generate the maze from the script; this approach has several advantages including: the possibility to create random levels, less time spent moving objects to create your maze, and the possibility to use algorithms that generate the maze automatically; so the next instructions will give you a heads-up on how this can be done.

To setup the environment, we will generate an indoor level using scripting.

We will proceed as follows:

- Create an array that represents the environment.
- Read the array.
- Instantiate objects based on the numbers read in the array.

So let's get started:

- Please create a new scene and rename it **gameLevelAuto** (or any other name of your choice).
- Create a new cube and rename it **ground**.
- Make sure that the ground **scale** property is **(100, 1, 100)** and its position **(0,0,0)**.
- You can also create a material for the ground if you wish.

Next, we will create an object that will be used to instantiate the walls.

- Create a new cube.
- Rename it **wall**.
- Set its **scale** property to **(10,2,10)**.
- You can also create and apply a blue **Material** to this object or use any other texture of your choice.
- Once this is done, you can create a prefab from this object, rename this prefab **wall**, and deactivate the object **wall** in the **Hierarchy** window.

Next, we will create a script that will generate our maze.

Putting it all together

- Create a new C# script and rename it **GenerateMaze**.

- Open this script and add the following code at the beginning of the class (just before the **Start** method).

```
public GameObject wall, player, npc_guard;
private int [,] worldMap = new int [,]
{
{1,1,1,1,1,1,1,1,1,1},
{1,2,1,0,0,0,0,0,0,1},
{1,0,1,0,1,0,1,0,0,1},
{1,0,1,0,0,0,0,0,0,1},
{1,0,1,1,1,1,0,0,0,1},
{1,0,0,0,0,0,0,0,0,1},
{1,0,1,0,1,0,1,1,1,1},
{1,0,0,1,0,0,0,0,0,1},
{1,0,1,0,0,0,0,0,0,1},
{1,1,1,1,1,1,1,1,1,1},
};
```

In the previous code:

- We declare three public **GameObject** variables that will be used as placeholders in the **Inspector** window to set the objects to instantiate with the corresponding prefabs.

- We then declare an array (two-dimensional array) of integers. The structure of this array mirrors the structure of the maze that we would like to create; for example the top row could be the north wall, the bottom row could represent the south wall, etc. So each value of **1** represents a wall, and each **0** represents an empty space.

- In its entirety, the array will represent the outline of our maze; the 1s represent walls, and the 0s represent empty spaces for now. Each row of the array is defined using opening and closing brackets with values within separated by commas.

Please add the following code to the **Start** method:

Putting it all together

```
int i,j;
for (i = 0; i < 10; i++)
{
        for (j = 0; j < 10; j++)
        {
              GameObject t;
              if (worldMap [i,j] == 1) t = (GameObject)(Instantiate (wall, new Vector3 (50-i*10, 1.5f, 50-j*10), Quaternion.identity));
              if (worldMap [i,j] == 2)
              {
                    t = (GameObject)(Instantiate (player, new Vector3 (50-i*10, 1.5f, 50-j*10), Quaternion.identity));
                    t.name = "FPSController";
              }
        }
}
```

In the previous code:

- We declare two integers **i** and **j**; these will refer to specific rows and columns in our array. For example if **i equals 1 and j** = 1, we will be looking at the row **1** and the column **1**. Because each array starts at 0, these will effectively be the second row and the second column in our array.

- We then create two loops; these loops will go through each row of our array.

- We then check the value of each element read in the array.

- If the value is **1**, we instantiate a **wall** prefab accordingly.

- If the value is **2**, we instantiate a **player** prefab (i.e., First-Person Controller).

Now, we just need to finish our setup as follows:

- Save your script.

- Check that it is error-free.

- Create an empty object and rename it **generateMaze**.

- Then drag and drop the script **GenerateMaze** to the object **generateMaze**.

- Once this is done, select the object **generateMaze**.

- Make sure that the **Inspector** window is active.

- Look at the parameter called **wall** for the script **GenerateMaze** attached to this object, and drag and drop the prefab **wall** to this variable.

- Drag and drop the prefab **FPSController** (ensuring it is the one that you have created in the previous chapters; this prefab should be located in your **Assets** folder and include the scripts **ManageCollisionWithPlayer2** and **ManagePlayerHealth**) to the variable **player**.

- Drag and drop the prefab **npc_guard** from the **Project** window to the variable **guard**.

- You can deactivate the object **FPSController** that is already in the **Hierarchy** (if any).

- You can deactivate the object **Main Camera** that is already in the **Hierarchy**.

- Finally, you can also drag and drop the prefab **UI** to the scene, so that you can see information on your number of lives and ammunitions.

- Once this is done, you can play the scene, and check the layout either from the **Scene** view or the **Game** view.

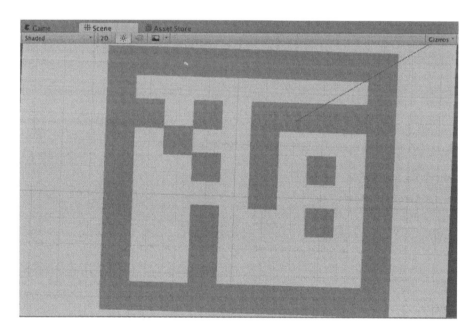

Figure 6-5: The maze viewed from above

Putting it all together

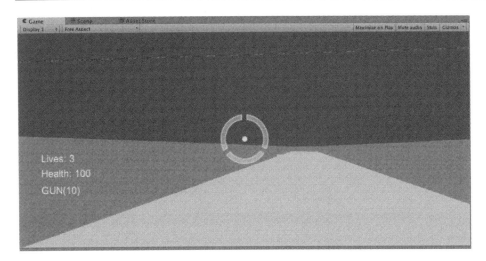

Figure 6-6: The maze viewed from the player's perspective

Next, we could try to add a few guards by modifying the script **GenerateMaze** as follows:

- Please modify the array as follows by adding 3s in places (you can add them where you wish).

```
{1,1,1,1,1,1,1,1,1,1},
{1,2,1,0,0,0,0,3,0,1},
{1,0,1,0,1,0,1,0,0,1},
{1,0,1,0,0,0,0,0,0,1},
{1,0,1,1,1,1,0,0,0,1},
{1,3,0,0,0,3,0,0,0,1},
{1,0,1,0,1,0,1,1,1,1},
{1,0,0,1,0,0,0,0,0,1},
{1,3,1,0,0,0,0,0,3,1},
{1,1,1,1,1,1,1,1,1,1},
```

- Also add the following code within the **Start** method, within the conditional statement (new code in bold).

[290]

```
for (i = 0; i < 10; i++)
{
        for (j = 0; j < 10; j++)
        {
                GameObject t;
                if (worldMap [i,j] == 1) t = (GameObject)(Instantiate (wall, new
Vector3 (50-i*10, 1.5f, 50-j*10), Quaternion.identity));
                if (worldMap [i,j] == 2)
                {
                        t = (GameObject)(Instantiate (player, new Vector3 (50-i*10,
1.5f, 50-j*10), Quaternion.identity));
                        t.name = "FPSController";
                }
                if (worldMap [i,j] == 3) t = (GameObject)(Instantiate (npc_guard, new
Vector3 (50-i*10, 0.5f, 50-j*10), Quaternion.identity));
        }
}
```

- Save your code.

- Check that it is error-free using the **Console** window.

- Select the object **ground**, then, using the **Navigation** window, select the option **Navigation Static**, and click on **Bake**.

- You can now test the scene.

- As a guard sees you, and possibly loses sight of the player, you may notice that it goes through the walls to reach its final destination. This is because, contrary to what we have done in previous chapters, we have not baked the scene (i.e., the walls), so Unity has not computed any of the necessary paths for the NPC.

- Unfortunately, at present there is no way to bake the scene at run time; however, there is a trick that we can use, that is, to add a **NavMeshObstacle** component to the wall component. By doing this, we ensure that the NPC will avoid the walls on its way back to the player.

So now you can do the following:

- Select the **wall** object in the scene and activate it.

- Open the **Navigation** window.

- Select the option **Navigation Static** and then click on the button **Bake**.

- The baking process is still necessary here so that the **NavMeshAgent** for our NPC finds its destination.

Putting it all together

- Once this is done, add a **NavMeshObstacle** component to the wall (**Component | Navigation | NavMeshObstacle**).

- Update the corresponding prefab by clicking on the button **Apply** located in the top-right corner of the **Inspector** window or by dragging and dropping the **wall** object to the **wall** prefab.

- You can now deactivate the **wall** object in the scene (since the prefab has been updated).

- Once this is done, please check the scene.

Once you have checked that everything works fine, you can start to add other objects, including med packs, ammunitions, or the objects to collect using the same array (or a different array if you wish).

LEVEL ROUNDUP

In this chapter, we have learned how to combine the skills that you have acquired to date in order to design a challenging level. We looked at reusing prefabs, and also generating a level automatically, and all of that using C#. So let's take a look back from the start of the book and appreciate your progress; you have learned to:

- Create C# code.
- Create classes.
- Apply C# in your scenes.
- Use rigid bodies.
- Create simple and more complex weapons.
- Create prefabs so that you can reuse relatively complex behaviors, objects and scripts.
- Create Finite State Machines (FSMs).
- Apply these FSMs to animated characters.
- Create realistic behaviors for NPCs whereby NPCs can detect the player using sight and field of view, and then walk towards and attack the player.
- Use relatively interesting algebra concepts such as **dot product** to simulate a field of view.
- Generate a level procedurally.

So, well, you have covered a lot and congratulations for reaching this stage of the book.

7
FREQUENTLY ASKED QUESTIONS

This chapter provides answers to the most frequently asked questions about the features that we have covered in this book. Please also note that some **videos are also available on the companion site** to help you with some of the concepts covered in this topic, including AI, UI, collision, cameras, or paths.

C# Scripts

How do I create a script?

In the **Project** window, select: **Create | C# Script**.

How can my script be executed?

As for JavaScript scripts, your C# script may need to be attached to an object. This being said, you could also create a class that is not linked to an object but that is used indirectly by another class (that could be attached to an object).

How can I check that my script has no errors?

Open the **Console** window and any error should be displayed here.

What is object-oriented programming?

In object-oriented programming, your program is seen as a collection of objects that interact with each other using, for example, methods.

Should the name of my C# file and the containing class within be the same?

When you create a new C# file, Unity will let you rename it straight-away; once this is done, it will automatically generate the name of the class within, using the name that you have specified for this file. So, if you happened to change the name of this file later on, you may also need to change the name of the class within.

Why should I use C#?

There are several good reasons to start coding in C#. One of them is that C# is an object-oriented programming language that is relatively similar to other languages such as Java. So by learning C# you should be able to transfer this knowledge to other languages easily.

What is the dot notation for?

The dot notation refers to **object-oriented programming**. Using dots, you can access properties and functions (or methods) related to a particular object. For example **gameObject.transform.position** gives you access to the **position** from the **transform** of the object linked to a script. It is often useful to read it backward; in this case, the dot can be interpreted as **"of"**. So in our case, **gameObject.transform.position** can be translated as "the position **of** the transform **of** the **gameObject**".

Rigid Bodies

What are rigid bodies?

Rigid bodies are components that make it possible for an object to be subject to the laws of physics, including gravity.

How can I add a rigid body to an object?

This can be done in several ways, including by selecting the object and then the menu **Component** (from the top menu) or using **Add Component** in the **Inspector**.

How can I add force to an object that includes a rigid body?

When an object includes a rigid body, you can apply a force to it, from a script, using the method **AddForce**; for example:

```
gameObject.rigidbody.AddForce (New Vector3 (10,10,10));
```

USING PREFABS

What is a prefab?

A prefab can be compared to a template that can be reused (and updated) indefinitely.

How can I create a prefab?

Just drag and drop an object to the **Project** window or select **Create | Prefab** from the **Project** window.

How can I add a prefab to a scene?

You can either drag and drop the prefab from the **Project** window to the **Scene** view or instantiate this prefab from a script.

Can I use prefabs across scenes?

Yes, since the prefab is saved in your project, it can be accessed from any scene within this project.

FINITE STATE MACHINES

How can I create an FSM in Unity?

You will need to create an **Animator Controller**. This controller will include states, transitions and parameters.

How do I link my Animator Controller to an object?

You can add an **Animator** component to this object, and then add the **Animator Controller** to this **Animator** component (i.e., drag and drop the **Animator Controller** to the variable called **Controller** for the component called **Animator** for this object).

How do I control my Animator Controller from a script?

- Add the script to the object to which the **Animator Controller** is linked to; then you can create a reference to the **Animator Controller** from the script, as illustrated in the next code.

```
anim = GetComponent<Animator>();
```

- You can then access parameters using **SetBool** or **SetTrigger**.

```
anim.SetTrigger("gotHit");
```

How can I know the current state of an Animator Controller from a script?

- You will first need to gain access to information about the **Animator Controller** using the method **GetCurrentAnimatorStateInfo**.

```
info = anim.GetCurrentAnimatorStateInfo(0);
```

- Then you can use this information to access the state.

```
if (info.IsName("ATTACK_CLOSE_RANGE"))...
```

NAVMESH NAVIGATION

What is a NavmeshAgent?

It is a component that you can add to an object so that this object can navigate "intelligently" around the scene towards a target while avoiding some obstacles.

Why do I need to bake the Navmeshes before the NPC can move?

By baking the **Navmeshes**, Unity computes possible routes that can be used by a **Navmesh Agent** to reach its destination, accounting for the obstacles. This is done before the scene starts so it doesn't need to be done while the game runs, hence, keeping performance high for the game.

Is it possible to bake the scene at run-time?

Unfortunately, this is not possible at present; this being said, you can use **NavMesh Obstacles**, which means that they will be avoided without the need to bake the scene.

8
Thank You

I would like to thank you for completing this book; I trust that you are now comfortable with scripting in C# and that you can create interactive 3D game environments. This book is the third in a series of four books on Unity, so it may be time to move on to the next book for the advanced level where you will learn more advanced features, including networking, database access, and much more. You can find a description of this book on the official page **http://www.learntocreategames.com/books**.

So that the book can be constantly improved, I would really appreciate your feedback. So, please leave me a helpful review on Amazon letting me know what you thought of the book and also send me an email (**learntocreategames@gmail.com**) with any suggestions you may have. I read and reply to every email.

Thanks so much!!

Made in the USA
Middletown, DE
16 February 2019